OAKWOOD LIBRARY OF RAILWAY HISTORY OL39

THE
WHITLAND & CARDIGAN RAILWAY

by
M.R.C. Price

THE OAKWOOD PRESS

First Edition published 1976
Second edition, with additional chapter, 1991
Third edition, revised chapter 15, 2021

ISBN 978-0-85361-751-8

Printed by
Blissetts, Unit E1-E8 Shield Drive, West Cross Ind Pk, Brentford, TW8 9EX

Bibliography

Llanfyrnach Parish Lore (1969): E.T. Lewis
The Whitland and Cardigan Railway (1962): C.F.D. Whetmath
Railway World: Volume 12 (1951) page 125: J.F. Burrell
Railway Magazine: Volume 98 (1952) page 481: J.F. Burrell
The Metal Mines of Southern Wales, G.W. Hall.
Great Western Journal: No. 30 (Spring, 1999): Stanley Jenkins, Chris Turner

Acknowledgements

The Public Record Office (British Transport Archives); The National Library of Wales, Aberystwyth; Pembrokeshire County Record Office, Haverfordwest; Pembrokeshire County Library, Haverfordwest; The Public Relations and Publicity Department, British Railways (WR); The British Broadcasting Corporation, Cardiff; The Historical Model Railway Society; *The Carmarthen Journal*. R. Bowen, J.G. Brennan, H.C. Casserley, Rhys Ap Elis, Mr & Mrs J. Ellis Davies, J.J. Francis, E.O. James, E.T. Lewis, J.K. Lomax, The Rev. W.R. Nicholas, A.L. Owen, V. Stephens, The Rev. D.W. Thomas, E.S. Tonks, CF.D. Whetmath, O. Williams.

The writer is glad to acknowledge assistance given in the preparation of the postscript by the National Library of Wales, The Great Western Trust and Mr P.A. Rance, Messrs R.E. Bowen, P.F. Claughton, the late E.R. Mountford, J.S. Holden, J.N. Slinn, T. David, D.G. Rogers, R.W. Davies, D. Davies, J. de Haviland, E. Phillips and A. James.

Title page: A GWR 0-6-0PT, No. 1666 has just arrived at Cardigan with the local branch service and a good number of passengers are disembarking. *D.G. Rogers*

Front cover upper: View of Cardigan Station. Courtesey T. David
Lower: No. 4557 pauses at Crymmych Arms with an 'up' train for Whitland, 17th August, 1962.

Published by
The Oakwood Press, 54-58 Mill Square, Catrine, KA5 6RD
01290 551122   www.stenlake.co.uk

Contents

Chapter 1	Communications to Cardigan before the Railway	7
Chapter 2	Industry and the Railway in the Taf Vale	11
Chapter 3	Building the Taf Vale Railway	17
Chapter 4	Incidents, Arguments and the Inspection: 1873–1875	23
Chapter 5	The Taf Vale Railway in Operation: 1875–1877	29
Chapter 6	The Early Years of the Whitland and Cardigan: 1877–1880	33
Chapter 7	In the Shadow of the Great Western: 1880–1883	41
Chapter 8	Construction and Reconstruction: 1883–1886	45
Chapter 9	The Great Western takes over: 1886–1890	53
Chapter 10	The Route Described	61
Chapter 11	Locomotives and Rolling Stock	91
Chapter 12	Lead and Slate after 1870	105
Chapter 13	Great Western Days	111
Chapter 14	Nationalisation, Decline and Fall	115
Chapter 15	Postscript	121
Appendix	Passenger Services 1910–1958	134
	Index	135

The seal of the Whitland & Cardigan Railway.
Swindon Museum/Thamesdown Borough Council

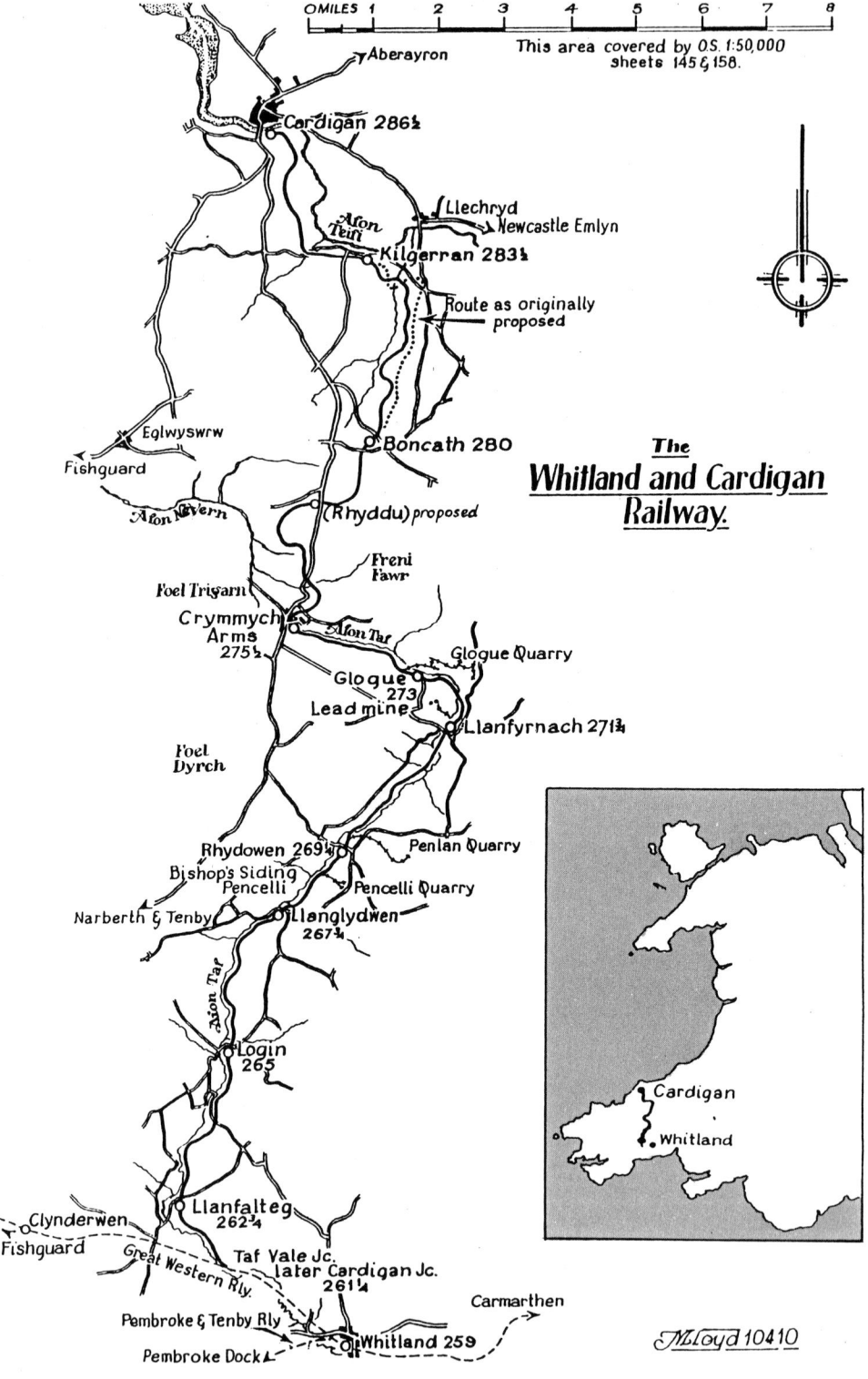

Preface to the First Edition

The 'Cardi-Bach' – the Whitland and Cardigan Railway – was an institution well loved in the valley of the Taf and in the villages north to Cardigan. The railway was a lifeline to remote hamlets and a means of prosperity for local industry. Even though it lost its independent identity as early as 1890 the line remained rather special to all those who knew it. Joining the train at Whitland there was an air of excitement and a sense of pioneering even in the line's last days. Steep gradients and innumerable curves kept speed down, but the long climb up the green Taf vale reached its climax when the train burst out of the deep summit cutting north of Crymmych Arms to wind around a long horseshoe bend across moorland on the edge of the Prescellys. If the run down to the river Teifi and Cardigan was less dramatic it was hardly less memorable: surely no one who ever took the 'Cardi-Bach' will ever forget it. Certainly the present writer owes all his interest to one such afternoon on the railway. On a day not long before closure a generous engine driver, cheerfully disregarding officialdom, offered a ride from Cardigan on the footplate of his '45XX' class tank. The ensuing 110 minutes were sheer joy, and if there is one reason why this small book has been written that is it. I must thank again that driver of the 'Cardi-Bach', and the many others since who have provided much assistance and information. A full list of acknowledgments appears on page 2.

Martin R. Connop Price
Cambridge, August 1975

Preface to the Third Edition

Almost 60 years after the closure of the 'Cardi Bach', memories remain remarkably strong. A Welsh language newsheet now appears in the district under the name 'Cardi Bach', and an energetic group of railway modellers and enthusiasts meet locally as the 'Cardi Bach Railway Society'. Their efforts, and support provided by the owners of the former station at Login, have enabled a small museum to be established on the site. Although the railway will not return to the valley of the Taf, the spirit of the steam age is reflected in the activities of the Gwili Railway, twenty miles away to the north of Carmarthen, on the route of the impecunious Carmarthen & Cardigan Railway (which never did reach Cardigan!). In their time these rural branches were of huge importance to the communities they served, and I hope this revised account may convey a fair sense of the Cardi Bach's significance in its own fascinating, but rather isolated area.

Martin R. Connop Price,
Ross on Wye, Herefordshire, September, 2020.

A fine view of Cardigan station, with an immaculate Great Western 0-4-2 tank locomotive, and a train comprising a horse box and four and six wheeled stock in brown livery.

Courtesy T. David

Chapter One
Communications to Cardigan before the Railway

The town of Cardigan has always been a rather isolated place, standing near the mouth of the River Teifi in West Wales and cut off by the Prescelly mountains to the south and areas of hill and swampland to the east. In spite of this the first proposal for putting Cardigan on the railway map was made as early as 1845, at the height of the Railway Mania. In that year there was a scheme to construct the Great North and South Wales and Worcester Railway, which included a line from Carmarthen to Cardigan and St Dogmaels. Not surprisingly, in that era of extravagant railway projects, the idea came to nothing.

At that time the roads over the hills from Cardigan were poor and lonely, and the town relied heavily upon its small harbour. However, as ships got larger and an expansion of trade appeared possible local people made efforts to improve inland communications. By about 1840 John Furlong of the Nantyddwylan Arms was travelling the road from Cardigan to Haverfordwest every other day with his covered cart. In the 1850s one Benjamin Davies operated a Royal Mail coach between these two points, the Union Inn at Pentregalar (two miles south of Crymmych) being the half-way staging post. The journey time at this date was rather less than three hours. By 1860 a coach drawn by a team of horses was functioning over this route, an inside seat costing 6s. and an outside seat 4s. In about the same year an omnibus service commenced between Crymmych and Newport, on the North Pembrokeshire coast, and this provided connections with the Haverfordwest coach at Crymmych.

By 1860 all those offering road services to and from Cardigan must have wondered how long their business would last: the railways were starting to make their presence felt in West Wales. Indeed in 1860, and also in 1863, Parliamentary Bills were prepared for a 'Milford, Fishguard & Cardigan Railway'. Although these came to nothing, the broad gauge South Wales Railway had reached Carmarthen from Gloucester in 1852. On 2nd January, 1854 it was extended 31 miles to Haverfordwest in Pembrokeshire, by way of St. Clears, Whitland and Narberth Road (later called Clynderwen). This line was doubled on 1st July, 1857, having been further extended to a terminus at New Milford (later Neyland) on 15th April, 1856. When the South Wales Railway was taken over by the Great Western Railway in 1863 it formed the backbone of the railway system throughout South and West Wales.

The company of greatest interest to the people of Cardigan was the Carmarthen and Cardigan Railway, formed in 1854 to build a broad gauge line from the South Wales Railway at Carmarthen to Newcastle Emlyn and Cardigan, together with a deep water port at Cardigan. The port was to be built by an associated company called the Cardigan Harbour Improvement Company, the pier and breakwater being located at Altycoed, near Cemaes Head, about five miles west of Cardigan. It seems that in the original plan the railway would have entered Cardigan along the north bank of the Teifi before bridging the river to reach St Dogmaels and the new harbour.

A contract for construction of the railway as far as Llandyssul was granted to Mr Jay of London by 1856, the Engineer being Joseph Cubitt. Initial progress was slow, and there were financial problems from the outset. In 1859 Cubitt advised the company to build the railway to the narrow (i.e. standard) gauge and it duly introduced a Bill into Parliament for the purpose. In the year of the death of I.K. Brunel, chief advocate of the broad gauge, perhaps Cubitt foresaw its eventual demise. However his recommendation was countered by the South Wales Railway, which became very anxious at the thought of a narrow gauge intrusion into its broad gauge domain. In due course the SWR agreed to work a broad gauge Carmarthen and Cardigan Railway at its own expense over the comparatively short stretch from the junction with the SWR at Myrtle Hill to Carmarthen Tin Works. On this understanding the Carmarthen and Cardigan Railway withdrew its Bill.

At this stage the Board of the C&CR took a step, which over a century later, seems almost bizarre. At the start of 1864 they had just over seven miles of operating railway: it became 15 miles 16 chains with the opening to Pencader on 28th March and 18 miles 58 chains with the completion of the section to Llandyssul on 3rd June. The effort involved in constructing this much was enormous, a 985-yard tunnel north of Llanpumpsaint being the main difficulty and reason for delay. Despite such exertions, and in the face of bankruptcy (which became actual in November 1864) the company sought, and got, powers for a line from the SWR at Kidwelly to Velindre, in the hills above the Gwendraeth valley. This place was at least eight miles from Myrtle Hill Junction, the nearest point on the C&CR, and yet in 1865 further powers were obtained to extend this separate railway to Pontyberem. Arguably the C&CR never intended to connect this new section with the railway running north from Carmarthen, but in any event a Receiver was now in charge of the company's affairs and in 1866 all these powers were transferred to the newly-formed Gwendraeth Valleys Railway.

The Receiver allowed the C&CR to continue running, but the outlook for the extension to Newcastle Emlyn and Cardigan became extremely dim. In the meantime, on 1st November, 1864 the Llanelly Railway reached Carmarthen from Llandeilo, and the 1 mile 75 chains from the new junction at Abergwili to Myrtle Hill became mixed gauge. Exactly two years later the Manchester and Milford Railway linked up with the C&CR at Pencader Junction, and the 13 miles 54 chains thence to Abergwili Junction was also converted to mixed gauge.

By now the broad gauge in South Wales was doomed, and the SWR's successor, the Great Western Railway, decided to convert all existing track there to the narrower gauge in May, 1872. This compelled the C&CR to do likewise, although as a result of the earlier work only 3 miles 9 chains between Pencader and Llandyssul needed conversion. This work was done at the end of May, and completed by 1st June, 1872, hired broad gauge locomotives and rolling stock being replaced by the appropriate hired narrow gauge stock. The peculiar feature of the whole operation was that Great Western services west of Gloucester had been worked exclusively on the narrow gauge since 12th May, and accordingly the C&CR somewhat unexpectedly had a claim to fame as the operator of the last broad gauge trains in South Wales.

In spite of all this activity, by 1872 one thing was obvious: the dreams of the C&CR were still far from fruition. Construction had halted at Llandyssul, and although in 1869 the manager of the C&C, Mr Tyler, floated another company with the object of building the extension, the local response was lukewarm. A meeting was held in Cardigan in October 1871 to consider means of raising the capital suggested by Mr Mackay, a contractor who had the backing of the famous railway builder Thomas Brassey. The proposals related to an extension as far as Newcastle Emlyn, and although the ordinary shares to be offered were reduced in cost as an incentive local folk were not in the mood to subscribe, believing that too much money had been squandered on such schemes in the past. One positive gesture at the meeting was a vote of thanks for Mr Tyler and his efforts to build the line to Cardigan. In 1869, though, it seems that Mr Tyler pursued his enterprise more vigorously because he was aware that the promoters of the new Whitland and Taf Vale Railway company were looking to Cardigan from the south. History was to justify his concern, but meanwhile the C&CR remained at Llandyssul. In 1881 it was leased to the GWR, and it was not until 1st July, 1895 that the line to Newcastle Emlyn was opened. The railway on to Cardigan was never constructed at all.

Cardigan station looking towards the buffer stops, photographed about 1910.
R.E. Bowen Collection

The Great Western Railway knew this station as Llanfalteg, locally it was known as Llanfallteg; the original postcard bears the date 18th December, 1912 and shows the angled level crossing in detail.
Courtesy R.W. Davies Collection

Chapter Two
Industry and the Railway in the Taf Vale

Whilst the citizens of Cardigan were watching the struggles of the C&CR, the proprietors of mines and quarries in the valley of the River Taf were conscious that the benefits of the line, even if built, would be minimal for them. The lead and silver mine at Llanfyrnach and the slate quarries at Glogue lay under the hills at the head of the valley, and the Taf ran south towards Whitland, St Clears and Carmarthen Bay. This was the natural line of communication, and the most usual route for the transport of slate and ore. By the late 1860s it was not enough to use packhorses to St Clears, Carmarthen and sometimes Cardigan: trade was on the increase and the time was ripe for a railway up the valley of the Taf.

Mining of lead and silver at Llanfyrnach had begun at least a century earlier. A survey of 1764 reported that the lead lay in a seam between 3 and 14 inches wide, and concluded with the encouraging comment that 'taking the whole together 'tis very plain that the adventurers cannot lose by this field if well-managed.'

By the 1850s the Llanfyrnach mine was of considerable size, and had levels at 10, 14 and 22 fathoms below the adit, or surface access shaft; but in 1861 the mining company succumbed to financial difficulties, and Llanfyrnach passed into the ownership of Thomas Turner of Wolverhampton. Employing several local agents he operated the mine for ten years, and this was a notably productive period. Two successful managers at the time were Mr Roberts and Mr Paull who, as men in charge, acquired the title 'Captain' in accordance with mining tradition. They enlarged the workings below ground and improved facilities at the surface, and the average output over the whole period of Turner's control was about 300 tons per year. G.W. Hall in his admirable book has also noted that when Turner wrote to Henry Gibson in 1868 he reported that the mine was in a first rate state for working by machinery on the surface, and for boring by machinery underground: the latter point is interesting because the date is an early one for the satisfactory use of rock drills.

In 1868 the lead mine was by no means the only industry in the valley of the Taf. At Glogue, about 1½ miles north of Llanfyrnach, slate quarries were in production, and they too had been in existence since the late 18th century. Records of the early years of this undertaking are extremely scarce, but it seems that unlike the Llanfyrnach mine the Glogue quarries were quite profitable early in the 19th century. The business continued to flourish, and it attracted a number of quarrymen from the more famous centres of the slate industry in North Wales. The slate was of the Ordovician period, durable, black in colour, or blue after polishing. The output met most local needs, and there were good markets for the product elsewhere. By the mid-1850s the slate was transported from Narberth Road on the newly opened South Wales Railway, or taken by barge from Blackpool, a tiny hamlet three miles west of Narberth, situated on the Eastern Cleddau. The arrangements served the purpose, but scarcely satisfied John Owen of Glogue Farm, the proprietor of the quarry.

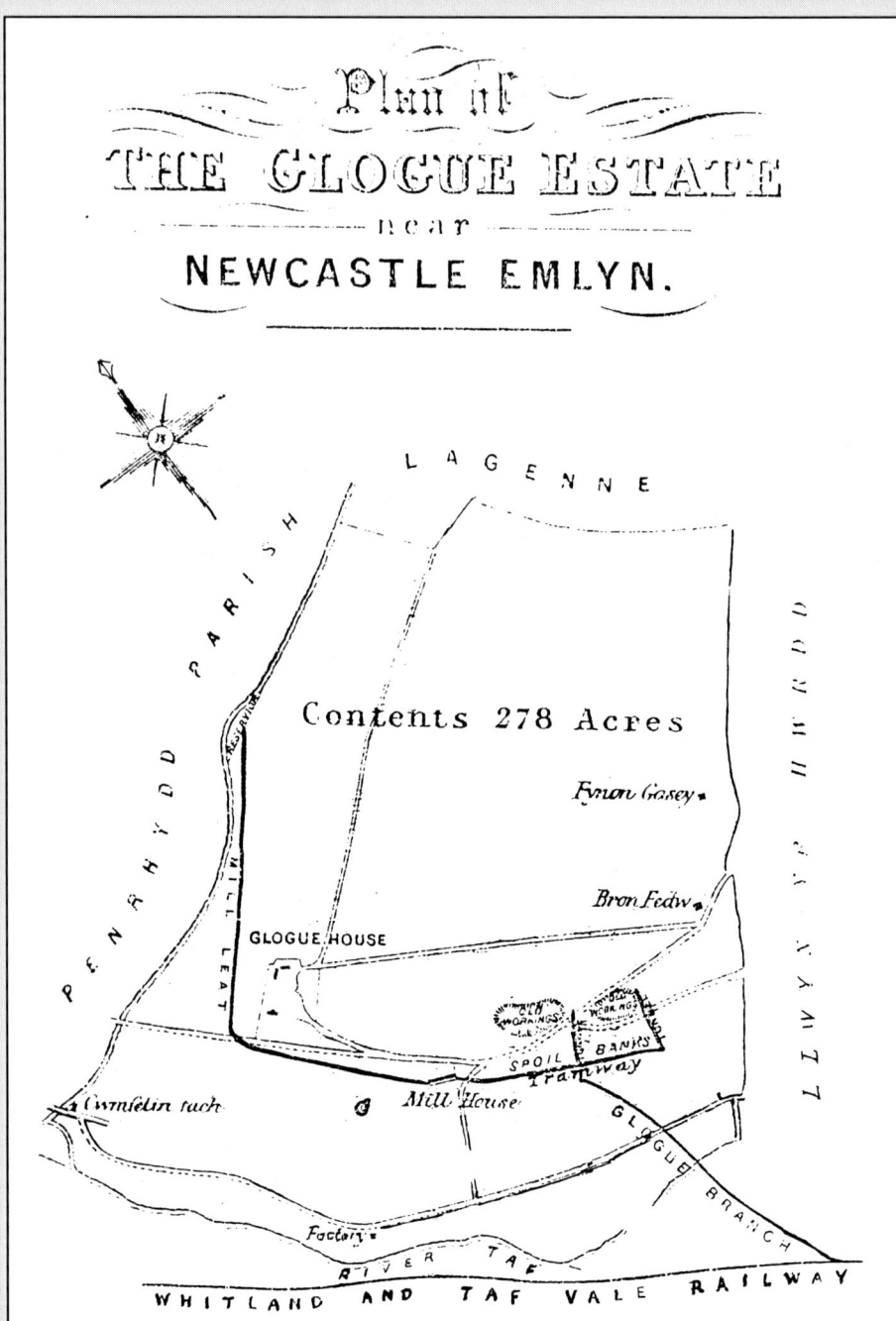

Glogue estate plan c.1875 showing the original branch coming off the Whitland and Taf Vale Railway.

Sir James Szlumper.
Courtesy National Library of Wales

John Owen of Glogue.
Courtesy Miss A.L. Owen

The Owens of Glogue were a large and adventurous family: John Owen had twelve children, three of whom emigrated to New Zealand. A fourth, born in 1818 and also named John Owen was deeply interested in education and for many years was involved in a successful drapery business in London. In middle age, however, he decided to devote his energies to running the quarry and to seeking to improve the economic conditions of the neighbourhood. Having succeeded his father as quarry owner, he was reckoned to be a fair and considerate employer. His greatest achievement, though, was his determined promotion of the Whitland and Taf Vale Railway; intended to provide a better outlet for the slate and minerals of the valley, it came into being in large measure as a result of his efforts. Although many others co-operated in the venture, undoubtedly he was the project's prime-mover.

By 1868 John Owen had entered into extensive correspondence with a young engineer, James W. Szlumper of Aberystwyth, about the possibility of building a standard gauge (4 ft 8½ in.) railway from Whitland, on the former South Wales Railway, to the quarries at Glogue and the main highway between Cardigan and Haverfordwest at the nearby hamlet of Crymmych Arms. By mid-summer, 1868, provisional agreement had been reached with Mr Szlumper regarding the works. In a letter from Aberystwyth dated 18th June, 1868, Mr Szlumper told Mr Owen that he would be ready to see to the construction of the line for a fee of £50 per mile, plus £15 per mile for out of pocket expenses. He also agreed to deal with the preparation of all plans and sections for the Parliamentary Bill, and to attend at Parliament for the passing of the necessary Act, if need be negotiating with any opponents. Probably at the request of John Owen, Mr Szlumper had taken the reassuring step of consulting the well known Welsh railway promoter, David Davies of Llandinam, who was 'pleased with the notion of making it a 4 ft 8½ in. gauge with the same weight of permanent way as 2 ft 3 in., using a 12 ton engine.' If so carried out Mr Davies also offered to subscribe £1,000 and provide all possible assistance.

At that date apparently neither Mr Davies nor Mr Szlumper had had a close look at the country between Whitland and Crymmych. It seems safe to surmise that Mr Szlumper at least did so later that summer, for the next recorded correspondence from him incorporates some revised terms but reveals no dampening of his enthusiasm. Writing to John Owen on 31st August, 1868, Szlumper offered to do all the work specified in the earlier letter, to make working plans and drawings and to superintend construction up to the opening day for a fee of £70 per mile, excluding all extras. He suggested stage payments of £20 per mile on the passing of the Act, with £30 per mile six months later and the remaining £20 per mile on the opening of the line. Owen was already deeply committed to the enterprise, but Szlumper proposed that his personal liability should not exceed £20 per mile, which amount would be the Engineer's total payment if the line was not made. John Owen decided to accept Szlumper's terms: the contents of the letters in due course became known in the company's Minutes as the 'Aberystwyth agreement'.

The relationship between the Whitland and Taf Vale project and the nearby Pembroke and Tenby Railway was interesting. There does not appear

INDUSTRY AND THE RAILWAY IN THE TAF VALE

to have been any formal link between them, but relations were definitely friendly. The Whitland and Taf Vale counted amongst its supporters David Davies, and William Owen of Withybush, Haverfordwest, both of whom were on the Board of the Pembroke and Tenby. In addition at one time the Engineer of the Pembroke and Tenby was none other than J.W. Szlumper.

Of the two undertakings the P&TR was senior by a number of years. It had extended its standard gauge line to Whitland from Tenby on 4th September, 1866 under powers obtained in an Act of 1864, and by another Act of 1866 the P&TR had authority to continue its line to Carmarthen which since 1865 had been the terminus of the standard gauge Llanelly Railway, approaching from the east via Abergwili Junction and the C&CR. This 1866 Act was an important move in terms of local railway politics, for it enabled the P&TR to enter into leasing and working agreements with the Llanelly Railway and its neighbour, the Central Wales Railway, both of which were under the domination of the very powerful London and North Western Railway. Faced with this sort of threat in territory it regarded as its own, the Great Western Railway agreed to grant running powers to the P&T between Whitland and Carmarthen. This was done by the P&T building a short spur line at Carmarthen and largely financing the complete conversion of the up track between Whitland and Carmarthen to the standard gauge. Although there was still a broad gauge line adjacent to it on the same formation, the conversion was notable as being the first on the GWR. Through P&T freight services to Carmarthen began to operate on 1st June, 1868, and a passenger service was introduced in August 1869.

This activity on the part of the Pembroke and Tenby was clearly important for the promoters of the standard gauge Whitland and Taf Vale. However they were busy enlisting support for the railway, and John Owen in particular devoted a lot of time to canvassing in the district. As good progress was being made with the legal formalities, on 3rd December, 1868, he was able to

Loading timber at Kilgeran station at the turn of the 20th century.

National Library of Wales

write to some potential shareholders advising that he had done everything necessary to ensure the passing of the Whitland and Taf Vale Railway Bill through Parliament during the ensuing session. He told them that a leading firm of London brokers would be placing shares in the market, but stressed that it was most desirable that 'a numerous subscription, however small, should be obtained from the locality, not only to give confidence to those who are not familiar with the resources of the district, but likewise to facilitate the passage of the Bill through Parliament.' Applications for shares had to be made before the end of the month in order to ascertain the amount subscribed in the county by then. Presumably the outcome was satisfactory, because early in 1869 the Act was passed unopposed enabling the W&TVR to be built as a light railway under the Regulation of Railways Act, 1868. Subject to the issue of the Board of Trade notice no locomotive could exceed 16 tons weight nor a speed of 16 mph.

The authorised capital of the company was £37,000 in 3,700 £10 shares. Five Directors were appointed, but somewhat surprisingly John Owen was made only Deputy Chairman. The Chairman was Stephen W. Lewis, a landowner and businessman of Regent Street, London. The other Directors were David Davies, Septimus S. Williamson, and Benjamin Evans of Cydigill, Cardigan, although it seems that William Owen was very soon made a Director in place of Mr Williamson. The company offices were at 123 Lammas Street, Carmarthen, and before long (July 1869) Mr Howell Davies was appointed Company Secretary. In the meantime the first formal meeting of the company took place at the Ivy Bush Royal Hotel, Carmarthen, on 9th February, 1869, and on this occasion the Board approved the terms agreed by John Owen in his correspondence with Szlumper. Detailed preparations could now be made for constructing the Whitland and Taf Vale Railway.

Directors, quarrymen and others at Glogue quarries photographed about 1925.
J. Ellis Davies

Chapter Three
Building the Taf Vale Railway

One of the first concerns of the new company was to negotiate with the GWR for laying in mixed gauge track from the station at Whitland to the junction with the Taf Vale line 2¼ miles west of Whitland. The possible cost of this facility was a matter of some anxiety, and the W&TV Board resolved to settle for a rent of £350 per annum or, if receipts from this portion were over £350, to pay the GWR the difference less 20 per cent to defray working expenses. This scheme anticipated that the GWR would undertake all works and maintenance on the mixed gauge section. Although it is recorded that the Whitland and Taf Vale Railway Act passed quickly and unopposed, in practice negotiations with the Great Western were tough. The Minutes of the W&TV note that on 15th April, 1869, when further discussion with the Great Western seemed 'hopeless', a meeting took place in the lobby of the House of Commons between James Grierson, General Manager of the GWR and Stephen Lewis, John Owen, J.W. Szlumper and Mr Bell (the Parliamentary agent of the W&TV) supported by David Davies. Evidently a vital Parliamentary Bill relating to works on the GWR was already under consideration, but that company was reluctant to accommodate the W&TVR. Discussion continued, though, and in this somewhat dramatic setting certain detailed amendments were agreed and arrangements for the junction settled.

The affairs of the new undertaking were moving ahead briskly. In April the Board was told that there were assurances that £9,000 worth of shares would be subscribed for, and that a large proportion of local landowners had consented to accept rent charges in respect of land required for the railway. Nevertheless from the outset the Directors had to be ready (and were ready) to dip deep into their own pockets to finance the project, and of £12,000 promised by the end of July that year the lion's share came from members of the Board. A Mr J. Barrow agreed to find another £5,000, and a loan of £10,000 at 5 per cent for five years was contemplated, upon the security of the Glogue slate quarries and the personal security of the Chairman and Directors. Such gestures leave little room for doubt about the commitment and confidence of the promoters. It was of course a confident age, and even after the stock market crisis of 1866, linked with the failure of Overend Gurney & Co., the mood managed to endure. The promoters were true Victorians, and the belief sustaining industry and empire was matched in microcosm by this remote railway company in Wales.

In the autumn of 1869 the Whitland and Taf Vale Railway issued a Prospectus encouraging the public to take up its shares at a deposit of £1 per share. In the best traditions of such documents it described the prospects of the new venture in glowing terms. In agriculture and minerals the district was 'extensive and rich' and the local roads were 'very bad'. Stress was laid on the virtues of inexpensive lines, and a rather vague but very optimistic comparison made between the traffic returns of the poorest lines in the kingdom and the potential returns of the new railway. With a little name-dropping – a not unreasonable reference to the acknowledged experience of David Davies – the Prospectus asserted that the entire cost of the works

The main street of Crymmych Arms at the turn of the century. *R.W. Davies Collection*

A general view of Login with the railway on the right. *Author's Collection*

would not exceed £2,500 per mile, and hinted at a dividend above £10 per cent on the whole capital.

So much for the hopes of the new railway: at the end of 1869 a very great deal still had to be done. In contrast to the Directors, a few local landowners with no direct interest in the line were anything but generous. By the time Szlumper had completed more detailed plans in the spring of 1870 negotiations to acquire the necessary land were becoming difficult. It is said that the toughest people the company had to deal with were ministers of religion, and years later John Owen remarked that had there been one more vicar landowner the scheme for the line to Crymmych would have had to be abandoned. At any rate, in August 1870 a report of the Directors was circulated amongst shareholders accusing some landowners of making exorbitant demands, and asserting that the company would not allow itself to be victimised by acceding to 'outrageous and impracticable demands on the part of those who (would) be first and most benefited by the line when made.'

Largely as a result of this development the Directors preferred a policy of not beginning construction until in possession of all the land required. Even so they were looking round for possible contractors, and before 1869 was out had contacted Mr Furniss, who had been contractor to the Burry Port and Gwendraeth Valley Railway. Within a few months negotiations with him came to naught, and the work was put out to tender. Five tenders were submitted and on 13th October, 1870, that of Mr Edward Lewis of Glandovey was accepted. He undertook to construct the railway to the Engineer's specification for £8,700, excluding fencing, which was to be an extra item. On consideration the Directors agreed to pay an additional £200 upon commencement, and £100 on completion to their satisfaction. The figures in this contract make remarkable reading when set against the estimate contained in the prospectus of the previous year!

Edward Lewis and his men started work on 8th November, 1870, and made rapid progress despite bad weather. The line was built from the southern end by gangs each working on half mile stretches. As portions were completed the material for and from the adjoining stretches was conveyed over them on tramways until the heavier rail was available and laid. When the Board met on 16th February, 1871, it was reported that the contractor had actually completed five miles of the earthworks and anticipated that mineral traffic to Llanglydwen bridge would be possible by early summer. On the other hand Szlumper stressed that much depended on the GW's willingness to make the junction near Whitland – and they were not obliged to do so until six months after the serving of a statutory notice. On the assumption that all would be well, Szlumper hoped that the line would be ready to Glogue by 1st May and to Crymmych before the end of the summer. Expectations were undoubtedly high! The Board had cause to be encouraged though, because by February, after prolonged negotiations, all the land had been purchased except for two pieces, the exorbitant claims for which were to be referred to a jury. Unfortunately at this moment the company's progress was checked.

In April 1871, the Chairman, Stephen W. Lewis, died, and soon after the prosperous Mr Barrow also died. He, too, had been a Director for a time. The new acting Chairman was William Owen of Haverfordwest, who may have been a relative of John Owen. In any event the Board now faced financial difficulties because although the cost of construction was said to be within the estimates, not enough capital had been subscribed. Probably as a result of money problems, construction work slowed down, but by the end of June the contractor had access to Whitland station, a temporary junction with the Great Western was installed and track-laying was in hand in the vicinity. However, the financial worries were becoming more serious, and in March 1872 the W&TV Minutes note with some sense of grievance that 'the works have not made such rapid progress as earlier led to expect'. Nevertheless trains had first reached Llanglydwen on 4th January, 1872, and Rhydowen on 3rd February, and the earthworks were finished to within 1¾ miles of Crymmych Arms.

At an Extraordinary General Meeting held on 13th April, 1872, it was stated that of the authorised ordinary share capital of £37,000 only £19,300 had been subscribed. To meet the deficit it was resolved to offer the remaining shares pro rata at £7 per share among the existing shareholders, any shares remaining being offered to the public generally. Shareholders were assured that the railway would be completed within the estimate, and informed that preliminary expenses, land and nearly all the professional charges had been paid for. Payment had also been made for the works then done, which included the laying of the permanent way from Whitland to the Llanfyrnach lead mines.

The works proceeded steadily, and by August the line was ballasted from the junction to Llanglydwen, and it was anticipated that on completion of ballasting to Glogue six or eight weeks later the permanent way would be ready for traffic. Hopes were rising again, and by the time the Board met on 21st October it was suggested that the line be opened for heavy goods 'as early in November as convenient'. Efforts were now made to obtain an engine, wagons and a brakevan, and it was decided to employ Evan Pugh as engine driver at 6s. a day. The fireman, Thomas Davies, was to be paid 3s. 6d. a day and the engine cleaner, Evan Thomas, 2s. 8d. a day. All three were to enter the company's service when the line was open for traffic, but significantly (in view of later events) there is no record of their suitability or experience.

During the autumn of 1872 there were fresh difficulties for the company. On 10th December the Board was told that 'frequent attempts had been made to throw the contractor's engine and wagons off the line by placing large stones theron'. Disputes had arisen with the GWR over the delivery of rails and fishplates in broad gauge trucks at Whitland, and also over the precise point that respective responsibilities for the junction began and ended. Luckily these issues were soon resolved, but more seriously relations between the W&TV and Edward Lewis deteriorated. The company's financial position was undoubtedly a primary factor, and whilst the surviving company records avoid awkward details, it appears that payments to the contractor were in arrears. Certainly when a date for opening the railway was proposed (for 14th January, 1873) Lewis refused to hand over possession of the line, and gave no reason. If the company had failed to meet its obligations to him a reason was hardly required, and it must be said that when the W&TV sought legal advice it was told it was not in a strong position.

The solicitor's advice might have provided a fair comment on all the company's affairs. The Directors had had to lay out large sums of money as the completion of the railway drew nearer, and they were becoming increasingly anxious to receive some income from the business. At a Board meeting on 11th February, 1873 they prepared a notice for Edward Lewis which more than hinted of desperation. They asked the contractor to give possession that day 'of the whole line finished and unfinished.' Lewis kept cool, and did not comply at once. In the meantime the Board had the consolation of knowing that the company's own locomotive had been delivered and was at work on the line. An 0-6-0 saddle tank engine built by Fox, Walker & Co., of Bristol for £1,600, it had been paid for and was 'perfect in every respect'. It was named after John Owen, as a tribute to the pioneer of the railway who became its Chairman on 1st March, 1872.

On 1st March, 1873, an ordinary general meeting of shareholders was told that although difficulties had delayed the opening, the hindrances had been removed and working would commence immediately from Whitland station to Glogue quarries via all intermediate stations. The locomotive recently purchased was then engaged in carrying materials for the sidings at the various stations. Sufficient wagons had also been secured (from the Bristol Wagon Co.) and the company was only awaiting the completion of the works at the junction by the GWR. Meanwhile Mr George Hall, station agent for the P&TR at Whitland, who had earlier been appointed 'clerk or guard' accompanying each W&TV train, had taken it upon himself to assume the airs of General Manager of the railway. In the view of the Board he had behaved himself 'so grossly' that he was summarily dismissed. A former station master at Narberth Road, Mr John Davies, was appointed in his stead, but only briefly until appointed station master at Llanfyrnach. Mr Benjamin Davies was then made guard at £1 per week.

Col Hutchinson, the Government Inspector, examined the junction on 15th March and suggested some slight additions. A Board of Trade certificate was issued stating that once these were made the junction could be opened. The matter was duly dealt with, and the railway was officially opened for goods and minerals on Monday 24th March, 1873. The usually reliable historian of the GWR, E.T. MacDermot, maintains that on this date the railway was opened only as far as Llanfyrnach. However the evidence available in the company's papers imply that the short section beyond to Glogue was opened at this time too. Certainly this is indicated by the reference to Glogue at the 1st March meeting, and it is clearly implied in the Minutes. The initial freight service consisted of two trains a day each way over the whole route.

Class '45xx' No. 4557 with a mixed goods train at Crymmych Arms station, 8th July, 1958.
H.C. Casserley

No. 4557 takes on water at Glogue whilst returning from Cardigan to Whitland 11th August, 1962.
Courtesy C.F.D. Whetmath

Chapter Four
Incidents, Arguments and the Inspection: 1873–1875

At about the time the railway opened the disagreement between the W&TV and the contractor came to a head. Under pressure from the company Edward Lewis eventually withdrew, but with some claims outstanding. In accordance with the provisions of the Aberystwyth agreement Szlumper arbitrated between the two parties, and he awarded Lewis £545 19s. 10d. The company issued a cheque for all but £100 of the sum on the spot, but Lewis would not accept Szlumper's verdict as regards his extras. Believing it was abiding by the agreement the Board was not disposed to make concessions, and Lewis began litigation. When the case was heard the judge found in favour of the company and the Aberystwyth agreement was upheld. Thus the contractor received the amount for extras assessed by Szlumper and no more.

With the departure of the contractor the W&TVR had to press on with all outstanding work itself. On 29th April the Board resolved that the earthworks from Glogue to Crymmych be proceeded with immediately 'by our present staff'. In the same month five small timber huts were ordered for temporary stations on the railway. The additional work seems to have stretched the staff to the limit: the next few months were certainly full of incident. On 3rd June some loaded wagons were let down the quarry incline at Glogue, but were not controlled by the brakeman. They ran on to the W&TV line and down the gradient to Llanfyrnach station, where they collided with several wagons, damaging two belonging to the company and two belonging to the Pembroke and Tenby Railway. The company's overman at Glogue, Mr David Roberts, admitted responsibility saying that his men had done as instructed and that it had been the practice to allow wagons to run all the way from Glogue to Llanfyrnach under gravity. On this occasion the rails were slippery with rain and the wagons were not checked. The practice was strictly prohibited thereafter.

On 19th July, 1873, there was an incident which was as comic as it was foolish. That evening Evan Pugh, the engine driver, and Thomas Davies, the fireman, quarrelled with the guard, Benjamin Davies, at Whitland. In furious mood the crew set off with the last freight of the day up the Taf Vale, but on a '1 in 50 incline' between the Great Western junction and Llanfalteg the locomotive was stopped and cut off from the train. The enginemen then drove off home leaving the guard, six loaded coal wagons and several other wagons stranded in such a position as to run the risk of the train running back on to the Great Western main line. How the guard coped in this remarkable situation unfortunately is not recorded! Suffice to say that the event was reported, and three days later John Owen found against Pugh and his fireman and dismissed them. New men were needed and David Rees, driver, and Thomas Elias, fireman, were engaged instead. Operations continued to have a somewhat 'wild west' air, though, for on 19th October large stones were placed on the track near Llanglydwen. The train was stopped just in time and a reward of £20 was offered for detection of the 'evil-disposed person'.

Building of the extension to Crymmych was going ahead, and to speed up the works it was decided to hire a locomotive for 12 weeks from the celebrated Mr Isaac Watt Boulton of Ashton-under-Lyne, at a cost of £150, exclusive of carriage. This engine was No. 1816 *Alma*, a 2-4-0 tender locomotive formerly of the London and North Western Railway. As the W&TVR had requested immediate delivery Mr Boulton went to Crewe in person on 23rd January, 1874, to collect his latest acquisition and convey it to Wales. In *The Chronicles of Boulton's Siding* A.R. Bennett tells how No. 1816 became pilot to the locomotive of a fast train, the driver of which decided to make fun of the smaller engine. He pushed it along at ever increasing speed despite Boulton's signals to slow down. Only when they were running rapidly down a bank which terminated in a sharp curve did the driver ease up, which was as well for safety and for No. 1816, which was beginning to run hot. Eventually the locomotive reached Whitland running light engine, but once on the W&TVR the company soon concluded it was unsuitable for use on ballast trains. In consequence it spent most of its time on the company's freight service whilst the 0-6-0 saddle tank *John Owen* was employed on the works for the railway extension.

According to A.R. Bennett No. 1816 returned to Ashton-under-Lyne in June, and although the company minutes make no specific mention of the hire being extended by two months there is no reason to doubt that this happened. If so the locomotive's departure must have co-incided with the completion of the railway to Crymmych. The precise date of the opening of the short portion between Glogue and Crymmych is not known, but it would appear to have been early in July 1874. In any event, in a report to shareholders dated 10th August, 1874, John Owen announced the completion of the line to the terminus at Crymmych and stated 'The line has been opened throughout the whole distance for several weeks for goods and minerals, with most encouraging results – the receipts having increased to more than double the amount previously taken.' Owen went on to say that the Directors had made arrangements with Mr Powlesland, contractor and carrier of the GWR at Swansea, for a daily delivery of goods at Cardigan where they had opened a receiving and delivery office. This agreement was effective from 1st August, 1874, and binding initially for three months. Soon after the company entered into another notable contract – with the Postmaster General. The contract was for five years from 1st October, 1874, for carriage of the London mails from Whitland to Crymmych, the distance to be covered in 70 minutes and the rate to be £200 per year.

Traffic was increasing handsomely: in the half year up to 30th June, 1874 receipts on merchandise and mineral traffic totalled £924 15s. 11d., but in the following six months the total was £1,503 19s. 5d. This increase in business put a strain on men and equipment, and it was possibly indicative of the situation that on 24th July the Directors were told that the fireman, David Elias, had lost a foot in an accident at Crymmych. The circumstances are not described, but the accident was attributed to mechanical failure, a broken spring on the locomotive being mentioned. The trains kept moving nevertheless, although in November a crisis arose because the traffic became so heavy that it kept the locomotive working almost night and day, 'until so far disabled that great delays were occasioned'. Fearing a complete breakdown, and being unable to convene a Board meeting the Chairman consulted several prominent shareholders and purchased another locomotive from Fox, Walker & Co. of Bristol. The price was £1,900, to be paid in 20 equal quarterly instalments.

The new locomotive, No. 2, was due to be delivered in January 1875 but Fox, Walker & Co did not oblige, apparently because they were not satisfied with the security offered by the company. By now locomotive No. 1 *John Owen* had broken down completely and the W&TVR had no option but to hire an engine from Mr Boulton's siding once again, and that possibly No. 1816, even though it had not been a great success in the previous year.

The W&TV Board was annoyed at Fox, Walker & Co's attitude over delivery of the second locomotive, and although the firm soon agreed to accept deferred payments John Owen was asked to press them for compensation in respect of the railway's loss and inconvenience. The Chairman did well, obtaining £125 in compensation and an option to purchase the engine outright for an additional £5 after five years from 1st January, 1875. Meanwhile Fox, Walker & Co. agreed to deliver the locomotive not later than 1st March. In fact it arrived on 10th March accompanied by the payment of a further £50 compensation by Fox, Walker's. Presumably as a consequence of the hire of an engine from Mr Boulton the new No. 2 was said then to be 'not very urgently required'. Be that as it may, more rolling stock was required. In the previous May four more wagons had been ordered from the Bristol Wagon Co., and as a result of the opening for goods to Crymmych an order had been placed in October for a covered goods van. By the winter of 1874 the intention was to open the whole railway for passenger traffic as soon as possible, and negotiations were begun with the Gloucester Wagon Co. for the construction of coaches: two composite and two third class coaches to be ready in the first week of May. The composite coaches were to cost £315 each and the third class coaches £210 each. They were insufficient and an order for two more of the third class variety was placed with the Gloucester firm.

Other preparations for the opening to passengers were well in hand. By December 1874 a tender had been received from Messrs Mackenzie Clunes and Holland of Worcester for signals and associated equipment, at Llanfalteg, the Blaenavon and Penclippen level crossings, Llanglydwen and Llanfyrnach stations, Glogue siding and Crymmych station. Six months later the Directors were able to confirm to the Board of Trade that the line would be worked by train staff and the Absolute Block Telegraph System. James Szlumper was evidently satisfied with progress, and on 29th May, 1875, he advised that the works were so near to completion that notice could be given to the Board of Trade in a fortnight. In fact it was exactly a month later that notice was given to the Board of Trade for the final inspection. Col Rich was appointed to carry it out, but he did not do so within the ten days provided by statute. The W&TVR Minutes sadly record 'The Chairman and Engineer waited for him specially at Carmarthen three days, and on the 10th [July] no communication whatever having been received from Col Rich, it was determined to open for passengers on the 12th, all the traffic nearly having been suspended for the inspection for several days.'

The account conjures up a vivid picture of John Owen and James Szlumper pacing the platforms at Carmarthen with increasing impatience before deciding in desperation to take matters into their own hands. Ignoring the Board of Trade the line was opened for passengers on 12th July, but in the meantime Col Rich wrote fixing 15th July for the inspection. It duly took place on that day. By now the Board of Trade had got wind of developments in West Wales and with impressive speed, even for 19th century bureaucracy, on 17th July wrote ordering the postponement of the opening to passengers for one calendar month. The object of this directive was to ensure that Col Rich's requirements were carried out, but once again the company turned a blind eye. As Szlumper shrewdly observed, because of the Inspector's mistake the railway had not been inspected within the statutory ten days and, by virtue of the passenger service run on 12th July, it had become an open line by the time of his visit. Accordingly the Board of Trade only had powers to recommend works and not to compel them. On the basis of this advice the W&TVR did not hesitate to go on running passenger trains whilst the necessary works were carried out.

In fairness to Col Rich it must be said that he produced his report promptly: a copy of it accompanied the letter from the Board of Trade dated 17th July. He stated that the line was 14¼ miles long from the junction with the Great Western, being built under a special Act specifying that no wheel should carry more than four tons and no train should go faster than 16 mph. The permanent way was described as Vignoles rail 3¾ in. high and 3¾ in. broad at the base weighing 50 lb. per yard and laid to transverse sleepers about 3 ft apart. The sleepers, which were half round 9 in. × 4½ in., were laid 2 ft apart near rail joints. The track was held to the sleepers by bolts, screws or dogspikes and the whole was well ballasted with waste from the slate quarries. The stations were described as small wooden sheds with a urinal and a platform, having home and distant signals interlocked with the points. There were seven level crossings of public roads and 49 underbridges or cattle creeps varying in width from 4 ft to 15 ft.

For a light railway Col Rich considered it 'substantially constructed', although the cost was comparatively cheap – about £3,000 per mile excluding land and rolling stock. According to Col Rich the steepest gradient was 1 in 40 and the sharpest curve of 12 chains radius, but the figures do not tally with the later plans and sections made when the Great Western Railway owned the line. Some discrepancies may be accounted for by the realignment and reconstruction which took place a few years later, but even then according to the GWR's plans there was a portion of 1 in 35 gradient on the approach to Crymmych, whilst a short curve north of Login was laid to an extraordinary 8 chains radius! In any event the Inspector wanted some improvements to be made, requiring lodges to be built at each level crossing, adjustments to crossing gates and some to the points and signals. He also desired a second platform to be built at the crossing places (in fact probably only Llanfalteg and Llanfyrnach apart from the terminus at Crymmych) the installation of station clocks and improvements in fencing.

There is a local story that even before the railway was opened for passengers it was possible for a person to ride as 1 cwt. or 1½ cwt. 'goods', depending on the person's statistics! This may be true, but the regular passenger service when it started was surely more comfortable. Initially it consisted of four trains from Whitland to Crymmych on weekdays only leaving at 6, 10 am, 12.15 and 7.35 pm. In the other direction there was a train from Llanfalteg at 5.30 am, reaching Whitland ten minutes later, and trains from Crymmych at 7.25, 10.20 am and 4.25 pm. The journey time over the 16½ miles varied from 1 hour 10 minutes to 1 hour 30 minutes. A road coach service to and from Cardigan connected with two trains each way at Crymmych, and another coach ran once a day to Newport.

W&TVR goods delivery wagon in front of the Guildhall, Cardigan.
D. Davies Collection

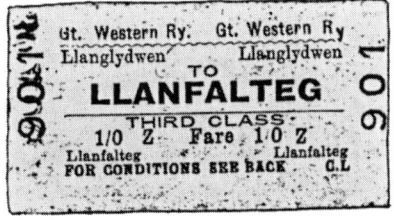

Whitland and Taf Vale Railway Company.

COMPANY'S OFFICES,
123, Lammas Street, Carmarthen,
26th March, 1872.

NOTICE is hereby given that an Extraordinary Meeting of the SHAREHOLDERS of the Whitland and Taf Vale Railway Company, will be held at the Ivy Bush Royal Hotel, Carmarthen, on Saturday, the 13th day of April next, at half-past 10 o'clock in the morning, for the purpose of authorising the Directors to issue the Unallotted Shares of the Company at £7 each.

By Order,

HOWELL DAVIES, Secretary.

SIR,

In the MATTER OF THE WINDING UP OF THE WHITLAND AND CARDIGAN RAILWAY COMPANY.

I have to inform you that the Agreement entered into between this Company and the Great Western Railway Company, and which was approved by your Company and Scheduled to the Great Western Railway Act, 1890, "for" (as stated in Section 47 of that Act) "amongst other things the vesting in "the Company of the undertakings of the Whitland Company and for the "appointment of a Liquidator of that Company as set forth in the third Schedule "to this Act," was thereby "confirmed and made binding upon the parties thereto."

This being so, the balance or the purchase money was paid on the 19th inst. by the Great Western Railway Company to me, as the Liquidator named in the Agreement, and at the same time I executed a conveyance of the undertakings to that Company.

It now remains for me to distribute the agreed amounts amongst the Shareholders, and I have to request you to fill up and sign the enclosed form, returning it to me as speedily as possible with your Share Certificate.

On receiving the form duly signed with the Certificate, I shall be prepared to give you a cheque for the amount payable to you in respect of your holding at the agreed rate of £2 per Preference Share, and £1 per Ordinary Share.

Yours faithfully,

Notices relating to the early history and the winding-up of the Whitland and Cardigan Railway.

Chapter Five
The Taf Vale Railway in Operation: 1875–1877

In spite of the somewhat fraught circumstances in which the railway was opened to passengers, the event was noted with approval by the local press, including the *Carmarthen Journal*. However that newspaper's report of the next half-yearly meeting of the shareholders revealed an interesting division of opinion between the local community and London bankers who held some of the shares. A representative of the bank said bluntly that his company wanted to improve its investment which was then in their books as 'a non-paying concern'. With a notable lack of realism the bank wanted the line to be continued to Fishguard to tap Irish traffic falling into the hands of the GWR at Milford. In reply John Owen evidently remained patient, and referring to the difficulty the company had met in trying to get support to build the line from Whitland to Crymmych pointed out that many landowners had only come forward to offer assistance on a promise of the railway proceeding to Cardigan. Any decision to branch off to Fishguard he felt would amount to the company breaking its word to these people. Although not surprisingly the bank representative failed to get his resolution adopted, he tried then to introduce more London men on to the Board. When this ploy failed as well he put forward a third and more enigmatic proposal – namely that the Directors should be paid 'if not to-day then at a future time'. The Chairman thought that this last proposition was 'slightly premature'.

Once the railway was open to all traffic everyday administration became increasingly onerous. Accordingly, on 28th December, 1875, the company's capable Secretary, Howell Davies, was also given the title of General Manager. Mr Davies, who had received a salary of £100 per annum as Secretary, now found that he was to be paid an additional £100 per annum (excluding travelling expenses) in respect of his new responsibilities. On the day of his appointment, however, the Board's attention was drawn to two matters the like of which were to be part and parcel of life for the new General Manager. Six days earlier at Whitland the GWR had managed to shunt a wagon into a W&TV carriage, nearly destroying one side of it. The necessary repairs were soon arranged, but the other problem took rather longer to resolve.

This concerned a claim in respect of a horse which broke loose and injured itself in a GWR horsebox when travelling near Carmarthen, *en route* from Crymmych to Hinckley, Leicestershire. As the Great Western had not loaded the animal it would not admit liability, and eventually well into 1876 the W&TVR decided to concede damages of £82 3s. 4d. to the owner to avoid the expense of defending the case any further. Such incidents apart, the General Manager and Secretary had meetings to attend, staff to see, and innumerable financial details to deal with – as the pages of the company's books bear witness. By now though a little prosperity was coming to the railway: it was decided to recommend a dividend of 3 per cent on ordinary shares for the second half-year of 1875.

The half-yearly ordinary general meeting was held at the Yelverton Arms Hotel in Whitland on 29th February, 1876. A report from the Board affirmed with great satisfaction that since the opening for passengers on 12th July 'the traffic has exceeded the expectations of your Directors,' and it went on to note that those outside the district had soon become aware of the line. Up to 31st December, 1875 the railway had carried 446 first class passengers, 949 second class and 17,085 third class passengers. In the same half-year receipts from passengers totalled £848 15s. 10d., from merchandise (including minerals) £1381 0s. 4d., and from mails £163 13s. 8d. After meeting all charges against revenue a balance of £1,020 12s. 4d. remained to the credit of the company. Accordingly, the recommended dividend was accepted and this took up £555 of the balance.

At the end of the next half-year the company was more cautious, for although passenger takings had gone up considerably the dividend was just 1 per cent. By way of comparison with the figures at 31st December, 1875, it may be noted that the receipts for merchandise and minerals in previous half-years were as follows: to 30th June, 1874 – £924 15s. 11d.; to 31st December, 1874 – £1,503 19s. 5d.; and to 30th June, 1875 – £1253 19s. 10d. To pursue statistics a little further, the company abstracts are interesting in showing that in both half-years of 1875 coal alone cost the W&TVR more than the wages of its locomotive staff. The total wage bill for the first half-year of 1875 appears to have been £413 2s. 2d., and for the second half-year £554 11s. 10d.

In the spring of 1876 John Davies, the first station master at Llanfyrnach, was granted a yearly tenancy of the Crymmych refreshment room and dwelling house at a rent of £20 per annum. The station at Crymmych, called Crymmych Arms after the nearby inn on the main road from Cardigan to Tenby, was already a focal point in the life of the small community. Indeed, the railway was the main cause of its growth, and at this time the pioneering atmosphere must have been tangible. In 1875 the station master had been appointed local postmaster, and by authority of the railway company a letterbox was set up on the waiting room wall. With the opening of the line to passengers, and the provision of a refreshment room, lonely Crymmych must have seemed mildly metropolitan in the minds of some local folk – at least just before the departure of up trains! However as the terminus of the line, and transhipment point for a great deal of merchandise, the station and yard were doubtless busy during much of the day. In addition the road coaches from Cardigan and Newport came and went from the station daily.

In June 1876 a persistent Board of Trade enquired if the recommendations made by Col Rich in the previous year had been carried out. Evidently at least some of them had not because the topic was dismissed in a few words in the Minute books, and no resolution was passed. The Board was much more interested in a letter dated 13th June from the Great Western's General Manager James Grierson to John Owen at Glogue. This set out terms for maintaining the connection with the GWR at Whitland, which were as follows:

   a) for user from March, 1873 to 30th June, 1875 – £679 station toll plus expenses on W&TV traffic
   b) from 1st July, 1875 the minimum of £450 per annum provided for under the 1869 Act, and monies above the amount subject to the minimum of 80% of receipts in respect of the 2¼ miles from Whitland station to the Taf Vale junction

c) also from 1st July, 1875 £300 per annum for the use of Whitland station, subject to six months notice
d) the W&TVR to continue to pay the actual expenses of maintaining the junction.

The terms were tough, but the W&TVR had little option but to accept. Some dark suspicions about the Great Western's intentions grew up as a result of this deal, but it is probably fairer to say that the men at Paddington were commercially-minded rather than determined to ruin the rural railway. Nevertheless the GWR was not exactly helpful: from 19th June, 1876 passenger tickets over the W&TV were issued by the Great Western at Whitland, but in 1877 at least the line was not even mentioned in the GW timetable.

The first significant steps towards extending the railway to Cardigan were taken in 1876. At a Board meeting held on 7th July one of the Directors, Captain Gower, produced tracings of a survey carried out by a Mr Hurst. The Chairman commented that Mr Szlumper was also preparing plans which would shortly be available, but for the present the company was not prepared to commit itself to the extension. In fact Szlumper's plans were completed very quickly, being laid before the Board on 22nd July. In the ensuing discussion the Board agreed that it was desirable to make the extension, but came to no conclusion on the question of whether it should be built by the W&TVR or by a separate company. For the time being the Secretary was instructed to get in touch with the Mayor of Cardigan, Asa I. Evans, who had promised to call a meeting in the town to promote the extension. The meeting was subsequently held on 7th September and a committee was appointed to canvass for shares and to ascertain the views of landowners on the route. At that stage it was understood that all the landowners 'were prepared to treat the extension with great and unusual liberality.' At least one man promised to give his land for nothing for the purpose! In such an atmosphere of optimism the Board then resolved to seek Parliamentary powers for construction of the railway in accordance with Mr Szlumper's plans. Subject to the approval of the Parliamentary agents, it was proposed that the name of the 'united' company become the Whitland, Cardigan & Newport Railway.

Whilst the Cardigan extension was under consideration further thought was given to obtaining a third locomotive. On 2nd February, 1877, the Board was told that the Chairman and Secretary had arranged for the purchase of an inside cylinder 0-6-0 tank locomotive from Fox, Walker & Co. for £1,350. This engine, No. 3, was delivered on 11th April, 1877, carefully inspected, and given two or three days trial before final acceptance. For the convenience of the company initially it was mortgaged to Mr Owen and two other Directors of the W&TVR, until they could be paid from new capital to be authorised under the Cardigan Extension Bill.

The Bill was drafted by February, 1877, and for revenue purposes it was proposed to divide the extension into three sections: Crymmych–Boncath, Boncath–Cilgerran, Cilgerran–Cardigan. A feature of the Bill was that the capital of the new line was to be kept distinct from that of the existing line, and that receipts and expenses of working were to be divided by mileage.

The capital for the Cardigan extension, which was not conceived as a light railway, was initially to be £41,000 in £10 ordinary shares, but the significant clauses in the Bill were those permitting the GWR to subscribe £10,000 of this sum. On the advice of the Parliamentary agents it was decided to change the name of the company to the Whitland and Cardigan Railway rather than the Whitland, Newport and Cardigan Railway. At the same time, at a Board meeting held on 16th February, the Directors affirmed the desirability of extending the railway to Newport and Fishguard. In doing so perhaps the Directors were still under pressure from the London bankers, because in view of the problems already encountered by the company (and often recalled by John Owen) it seems hard to believe that they were really serious. In any event the discussion concluded with the Board resolving to promote a Parliamentary Bill for such an extension in the next session 'provided the company is not liable for any expenses attending the promotion.' There is no indication that the scheme was given any further consideration, and the Directors undoubtedly felt that one Bill was enough for that Session. The Bill went through its stages promptly, meeting little opposition. Accordingly the Whitland and Taf Vale (Cardigan Extension) Railway Act of 1877 passed into law, and the company became known as the Whitland and Cardigan Railway.

An Edwardian postcard of Crymmych Arms and the busy station area.
Author's Collection

Chapter Six

The Early Years of the Whitland and Cardigan: 1877–1880

The company's papers suggest that as early as 1876 the Directors may have realised that their railway was eventually likely to become part of the Great Western, but it must be doubtful whether many of the shareholders were then aware that the 1877 Act was to be the thin end of the GW's wedge. On the face of it little had changed: the line was going on to Cardigan and apart from a little help from Paddington the finance would come from the district. There is no indication that the Directors dissembled in the matter: much closer association between the Whitland & Cardigan and the GWR was not discussed by the Board for another two years, when most of the talk was about the Great Western working the trains when the line to Cardigan was complete. Accordingly as the Cardigan canvassing committee set about its task it was probably firm in the belief that it was backing a local concern. At any rate by November 1877 the committee was able to say that it could get share subscriptions amounting to £10,070, and that it hoped to raise a further £8,000 to £10,000. With Szlumper's approval the Board replied that when subscriptions of £18,000 to £20,000 were assured they could pledge themselves to build the extension to Cardigan. All agreed that the canvass should be pressed to an early conclusion.

In the meantime operations on the railway were marred by some unfortunate incidents. On 22nd June, 1877, a woman was killed near Llanfyrnach station whilst attempting to cross the line ahead of the oncoming up mail train. No blame attached to the driver, who sounded the whistle and tried to stop the engine before it hit her. Although all the authorities were informed, rather surprisingly the coroner did not hold an inquest. If the fatality was the feature of this event, inconvenience was the chief outcome of another accident involving the up mail (4.25 pm from Crymmych) a few months later. This mishap took place between Llanfyrnach and Rhydowen, and concerned a mechanical failure on engine No. 1 *John Owen*. Instead of sending the fireman to telegraph for help, the guard and the engine crew spent over three hours trying to carry out their own repairs whilst the irritated passengers looked on. The driver was not trained as a fitter and only managed to make the damage worse! Eventually at 10.47 pm the rescue engine arrived from Llanfalteg, and at 11.41 pm the passengers reached Whitland after the longest recorded journey from Crymmych. As a consequence of this episode the driver and guard were severely reprimanded, the locomotive had to be thoroughly overhauled and the company had to compensate three of the people delayed for their out of pocket expenses.

There was an additional lesson in this affair, as Mr Howell Davies observed: it showed a need for the telegraph to be installed at more points than just Crymmych, Llanglydwen and Whitland Junction, and that it was especially necessary at Llanfalteg where the engine shed was situated. The Board agreed, and the telegraph was installed at Llanfalteg and Llanfyrnach in 1878.

The establishment of the telegraph at Llanfalteg was only one manifestation of the place's importance in the working of the railway. Presumably the GWR was either unwilling to have the company's engines stabled on its property at Whitland, or demanded some exorbitant payment. So far as is known from the outset the company provided its own locomotive facilities at Llanfalteg, the nearest convenient point to the junction. The site was not large and the stone-built engine shed accommodated one engine and a workshop. The original track layout is uncertain, but it cannot have comprised more than a passing loop on the railway with two or three sidings for rolling stock adjacent to the shed. No reference has been found to any other locomotive depot on the line at this time, but it seems most probable that at least one engine was regularly kept at Glogue or Crymmych where so much of the company's business was done.

At a Board meeting held in Cardigan on 22nd April, 1878, it was reported that subscriptions for the Extension totalled £14,150. Although the Directors were still reluctant to start construction before the figure reached £18,000, hopes were sufficiently high for them to take up a bargain offer of 1,000 tons of rails at 80s. per ton. It might be more accurate to say that civic hopes were so high: the Board was prevailed upon to move *en masse* from their meeting place in a hotel to the Guildhall, where the Directors eventually gave an undertaking to make the entire line from Crymmych to Cardigan, and to begin building the line immediately at both ends. Perhaps a little mayoral liquor as well as mention of more probable subscriptions assisted in producing this undertaking, but the purchase of the rails apparently became a symbol of the company's readiness to fulfil it. Unfortunately in due course they proved to be as much a problem as an asset.

In spite of these events work on the extension did not begin at once. Delay in the purchase of the land was the chief difficulty, and during the summer Mr D.G. Davies of Cardigan was especially obstructive. For a time it was thought that the line would have to be diverted over the river Teifi to a terminus in Cardigan near the Priory – a proposal providing a reminder of the original Carmarthen and Cardigan Railway scheme of 1853 which sought to build a line along the north bank of the Teifi to Cardigan, before crossing the river to terminate at a new pier near Cemaes Head. Fortunately the notion did not have to be followed up, because Davies was persuaded to co-operate – at a price. Davies received £1,000 in paid-up shares and certain additional sums; he also retained the freehold in most of his lands and a right to build adjacent to the line. As a result of this and some lesser snags no construction work on the extension took place before August 1878. The purchase of the rails was completed however at the 'unprecedented low price of £3 12s. 6d. per ton' and the whole consignment (now 1,200 tons) was stacked at Crymmych and Cardigan.

At this time traffic on the existing line was said to have suffered from a period of economic depression, and hence income in the first half of 1878 was £100 less than in the corresponding half year of 1877. However, whilst in 1876 and 1877 business at Llanfyrnach lead mine was exceedingly bad, after 1878 it boomed – a fact doubtless reflected in the then much improved figures for mineral and merchandise traffic. One half-year of 1879 provided an income from passenger traffic of £970, the sum being derived from the sale of 412 first class tickets, 1,344 second class tickets and 20,739 third class tickets. Taking merchandise and mineral traffic into account the total receipts for the half year were £2,650 6s. 7d. Although the figures were fair, the company was still very far from being wealthy, and as ever the Directors looked to the Cardigan extension to produce the desired additional traffic. It was a little ironic that whilst that line was hardly begun the Board of Trade was continuing to fret about the railway to Crymmych: on 27th August, 1878, Col. Rich carried out a further inspection. Evidently his report was unexceptional because it was laid before the Board without comment ten days later.

By the autumn relations between Szlumper and the Board had deteriorated markedly. At the beginning of October the Engineer withdrew his assistant from superintending the works at Cardigan and the making out of pay sheets, and a Mr David Roberts was made acting superintendent instead. The Minutes disclose that Szlumper had sent an 'intemperate' letter to the Chairman with reference to his duties as Engineer. The Board felt that his complaint was based on a misapprehension of the facts and asked him to withdraw the letter, which had 'naturally pained our Chairman and works against the harmonious working of our Board'. A month later Szlumper had neither replied nor certified the pay sheets for the extension works, but three months later, at the Board meeting of 3rd January, 1879, a terse letter from him was produced. In it he asked if the Directors of the Whitland and Cardigan Railway intended 'to proceed with the Extension in a proper manner and so put an end to the great and unreasonable delay' which was still taking place. The reply was brief: the Directors were carrying out the works in the only way possible and would use all means at their disposal for the purpose.

Early in 1879 the question of the coach service between Newport and Crymmych came to the fore. The service which had operated from 1875 had been discontinued and no one had been found to re-open it. The matter was serious because in summer months it brought considerable traffic to the railway. However Captain Davies of the Commercial Hotel, Newport, now declared his willingness to run the coach provided the company or its representative joined in with him. Accordingly it was agreed that John Davies of Crymmych should participate on behalf of the railway, and the company agreed on a temporary basis to provide half the capital required for the venture up to £200. Evidently John Davies was a man of some ability and education, for at this time his star was plainly in the ascendant within the Whitland and Cardigan company. Not only was he entrusted with many responsibilities at Crymmych, but he was given the additional title of traffic inspector. In this capacity he was required to visit local fairs and markets and to travel up and down the line to canvass for traffic.

In January 1879 Szlumper submitted more plans, sections and drawings for the new extension, but the accompanying report on the works was not adopted by the half-yearly meeting of shareholders held on 25th February. Instead approval was given to the action of the Directors in asking the

Engineer to examine the works again. Szlumper was displeased, and would not co-operate adequately with the company. A month later, having failed to resolve the problem, the Board decided not to ask Szlumper to certify any more pay sheets, nor to seek reports on the works under his superintendence. In effect this decision brought work on the extension to a standstill. Rather surprisingly the Board went further, and put itself on doubtful ground by telling Szlumper that his charges would not be met whilst a case against some defaulting shareholders of the Extension railway was pending.

If this behaviour was less than fair to Szlumper it may be a measure of the somewhat parlous state of the company's finances and the Board's anxiety about the cost of litigation. In any event by May Mr Barker, the company's solicitor, was advising on the issue, and in order to resuscitate the Cardigan project it was resolved to ask for Szlumper's loyal concurrence with the Directors, both he and David Davies M.P. being present if possible. Both attended the meeting which was held on 8th May at the Black Lion, Cardigan. Unfortunately Szlumper and the Board failed to settle their differences, and subsequently Howell Davies wrote to Szlumper to tell him that his position as Engineer was to cease, and that he should notify the company of his claims against it for past services. David Davies had suggested this approach to the problem, thinking it would also suit Szlumper, but when he replied on 3rd June he simply declared his readiness to continue to act as Engineer until dismissed. For some reason the company's response was not immediate, but when it came it was predictable; on 1st August the Board resolved to remind Szlumper of their earlier resolution, and to express their regret that he had not understood their previous letter.

The same Board meeting was noteworthy for another reason: John Owen now reported that discussions were taking place with the GWR about the working of the line by the Great Western, and the carrying on of the extension from Crymmych to Cardigan. No definite arrangements had been made because the GWR had seized the opportunity to press for payment of the balance of £3,800 due to them under the traffic agreement between the two companies. The demand embarrassed the Whitland and Cardigan not a little: as the extension works were suspended there was no real hope of making payment in shares, and the Board could only hope to reach some reasonable agreement in correspondence with the Great Western's Chairman, Sir Daniel Gooch. As if this was not enough, David Davies was seeking repayment on his £14,000 holding of debenture bonds, and James Szlumper submitted claims against the Whitland and Cardigan and the Cardigan Extension Railways to the tune of £2,700. The pressure was on the company, and at the half-yearly meeting of 26th August it was decided to start legal proceedings against two small groups of shareholders who had not answered calls for share payments.

In spite of these difficulties building the extension was still top priority. At a Board meeting held on 3rd October, 1879 it was reported that the contractors, Messrs Appleby and Lawton had offered to complete the works from Crymmych to Cardigan subject to a fresh survey of the line. In their view several important changes might be made in the route permitting a large saving in costs, and yet enabling a better line to be built. Not objecting to possible economies, the Board agreed to a new survey not exceeding £140 in cost. A letter was also sent out to local landowners advising them that the contractors had made a 'liberal offer' and that its acceptance would depend entirely upon the terms they were ready to accept for the land.

In the same month Mr J.B. Walton of 9 Great College Street, Westminster, was appointed Engineer until the extension had passed the Board of Trade inspection. For this service he was to be paid £1,500, half in cash and half in ordinary shares. The appointment was interesting because not long before Mr Walton had been made Engineer of the recently promoted Rosebush and Fishguard Railway, a line providing for the westward extension of the Maenchlochog Railway to the coast. Significantly the contractors for that concern (which together with the Maenchlochog Railway became the North Pembrokeshire and Fishguard Railway in 1884) were none other than Messrs Appleby and Lawton of Milford Haven.

On the Cardigan Extension Railway Mr Walton was given general superintendence of the contractor's work as well as responsibility for the new survey. In the event it seems that he recommended a new alignment only over the section between the villages of Boncath and Cilgerran, a proposal possibly governed as much by an awareness of the need for its Parliamentary authorisation as by considerations of civil engineering. Not only did it allow some work to go ahead at Cardigan and Crymmych whilst the new alignment was discussed by the lawyers, but the fact that the alteration was so limited may be taken as a sign that by this date the Whitland and Cardigan was not entertaining the idea of building branches to either Newport or Fishguard. Walton was already dealing with the latter wearing his other hat as Engineer of the Rosebush and Fishguard Railway!

On the basis of Walton's survey Appleby and Lawton wrote to John Owen setting out afresh their terms for undertaking the construction of the Cardigan extension. They offered to execute the works (including all earthworks, the making of two level crossings and four stations, and the erection of two signals) and also to maintain the completed line for six months for a total of £48,000. They requested payment of £30,000 in cash, £10,000 in debentures and £8,000 in fully paid up shares. The Board swiftly accepted subject to the committee at Cardigan increasing the subscriptions from the town and district from £15,000 to £25,000. The committee agreed to try to do this in a month, but early in December the Board was told that only £5,000 more had been raised and that no more than £1,000 extra was likely to be forthcoming. In the circumstances Appleby and Lawton offered to enter into a preliminary agreement to prepare two heavy cuttings at Crymmych and near Cardigan at the same price per cubic yard as that to be quoted in the main contract.

In spite of this helpful proposal the Board was hesitant, and consulted interested parties once again. Mr Appleby then said that he thought he could dispose of an additional £18,000 worth of ordinary shares at 30 per cent discount. The Board accepted his idea, but within a month Appleby had had time to reflect, and reported that he had not disposed of the shares and did not expect to do so. In the face of continuing pressure from bankers, creditors and their respective solicitors the Board decided to consult any other contractors likely to assist.

At this time Szlumper's claim was a sizeable problem. David Davies M.P. was reluctant to intercede any further between the company and its former Engineer, and instead suggested that if Szlumper was asked he would be reasonable in allowing more time for the company to pay the claim. Whether asked or not Szlumper obtained judgment against the company on 14th February, 1880, and on 16th February the rails for the extension were seized by the Sheriff in lieu of payment. This action was promptly contested, because the rails belonged to several Directors and not to the company as such. Rather than sell them to meet the debt it was decided to raise a loan for six months in order to settle with Szlumper. When his claim was eventually dealt with in March it cost the company £1,756 19s. 3d., with costs. As the W&CR's half-yearly revenue account showed a deficit of £635 10s. 7d., and the total deficit was over £900, this was not an easy matter.

The report of the Directors at the half-yearly meeting held on 27th February, was gloomy. In the past half year traffic had suffered from the general decline in trade, most especially felt in agriculture. Compared with the receipts for the second half-year of 1878 there was a drop in 1879 of £196 19s. 3d. The Directors could only hope for a local revival of trade matching that being seen in manufacturing districts. On the capital side the situation was not much more encouraging: Cardigan had offered only half the amount anticipated from the town to build the extension, and the landowners had not provided the support expected either. A fresh appeal was put out to them. In the meantime, although Szlumper's claim was about to be met, the Great Western was pressing for its December payment. The Whitland and Cardigan was in deep water on its current account commitments, and the overdraft was so serious that, in the words of the Minutes, 'it became necessary to pay the Great Western account for several weeks, with the consent of the Committee of Directors, by cheques received at the stations and not in the regular way by cheques drawn on the company's revenue account . . .'

The regular payment of rent charges on land comprising the original line was another problem, and in addition the Parliamentary Agent was pressing for the balance of his fees in obtaining the Extension Act. In such circumstances savings were vital, and in June 1880, the Board approved a reduced scale of wages for the men on the railways. The men quickly petitioned, but the Board saw no reason to change the policy: the reduced scale was comparable to the wages paid on other local lines.

Efforts were continuing towards purchasing land for the extension, and in the meantime James Grierson of the GWR offered some encouragement: he said that his company would offer to assist in relaying the existing line with rails of 72 lb. per yard and new sleepers. The estimated cost was £14,000, but although the Great Western would help to find the money at 4 per cent interest the company was not anxious to execute the work itself, or to work the railway whilst it was being relaid. The snag lay in the GW's desire to have priority of charge over all other stockholders, including the debenture holders.

With obvious reluctance the Directors agreed to put the point to the debenture holders, on the understanding that the GWR should not be given priority until satisfactory guarantees were given that the extension to Cardigan would be carried out, and a contract for the work signed. In the event it appears that the proposal was approved, because later the GW did contribute towards the relaying. Certainly at this stage the negotiations with the GW were becoming well known, and proceeding with the extension was the prime concern of all involved, perhaps as much to keep faith with the railway's supporters as to acquire additional traffic.

Negotiations with the GWR were not unconnected with the issuing of a Prospectus inviting the public to take up the remaining £26,000 worth of shares authorised by the Act of 1877. This shows that although the capital authorised was £41,000, an increase of £15,000 was proposed. Mentioning that the GWR was to subscribe £10,000 and the Cardigan district £20,000 the Prospectus explains that the capital of the extension was to be separate from the capital of the original line and that 'the receipts and expenses of working shall be divided by mileage.' Reference was also made to the rails already acquired, and it was optimistically asserted that whilst the average cost of railways in England was 'about £36,000 per mile the total cost of this railway including land, conveyance, engineering, and proportion of Rolling Stock, will scarcely exceed £6,300 per mile as a going concern.' The most illuminating comments, however, were upon the present and future traffic of the W&CR. After a reminder of the four coaches running daily between the railway and Newport, St Dogmaels and Cardigan, and the daily wagon service between Cardigan and Crymmych, the Prospectus pointed out that 'in a year of great depression the original railway carried over 45,000 passengers, and goods and minerals amounting to £3,000. The population of the district which will be served by the Extension is from 15,000 to 20,000. It is, therefore reasonable to expect that the passenger traffic will be at least trebled.'

Even then the assertions must have seemed ambitious. Fifteen to twenty thousand people, on the best estimate! That was the foundation for the scheme to build the 11 miles of railway to Cardigan. Considered almost a century later the enthusiasm of the railway promoters seems touching and quaint, but there can be no doubt that they believed in what they were doing and worked hard for its achievements. The profits might accrue to the businessmen, but the benefits would accrue to the community at large. The mineral traffic, it was said, would consist of lime, coal, slates and lead ore. Referring to the first the Prospectus mentioned that the Whitland and Pendine Railway would 'pass through the Marros Lime Rocks, about five miles from Whitland, and open up an abundant supply at very reduced prices.'*
Coal would also have to be distributed by the railway, whilst lead and slates were already sent to all parts of the kingdom in large quantities.

On this theme the Prospectus mentions that the two new slate quarries at Pencelli and Penlan were then opening, whilst the quarries at Cilgerran were in 'full work'. The Llanfyrnach lead mines were 'most productive' and

---

* The Whitland, Cronware and Pendine Railway obtained an Act in 1877 for a line about seven miles long from Whitland to Marros Lime Rocks and Pendine, on the coast. The anticipated traffic was stone and lime, but the project did not proceed for want of finance. A further Act was obtained in 1882 authorizing a line of 1 ft 11 ½ in. gauge, explicitly chosen for economy following the precedent of the Festiniog Railway. The railway to Pendine was never actually constructed.

further development was anticipated when the extension opened to them the port of Cardigan and the prospect of shipping ore at reduced cost. The latter was a point of general importance because the opening of the extension would give the advantage of lower charges for conveying certain classes of goods provided by coastal shipping. In addition the promoters looked for an increase in timber and fish traffic, and spoke of a new cattle market to be opened at Cardigan on the completion of the railway. The Prospectus' conclusion was quite in keeping with all these hopes: 'Large Trunk Railways, on account of their great cost and expensive working, do not pay the dividend which investors have a right to look for, but a Railway substantially constructed at one-sixth the average, and running through a populous district [sic], when economically worked, should pay a good dividend.' Suffice to say that the present writer has found no evidence that the Whitland and Cardigan, whilst it was so called, ever paid a dividend of any kind, at least on its Ordinary shares.

A Great Western saddletank, believed to be number 1962, at Cardigan with a mixed train. *T. David Collection*

348.—WHITLAND AND TAFF VALE.

Incorporated by 32 and 33 Vic., cap. 91 (12th July, 1869), to construct a railway from the South Wales section of the Great Western, near Whitland, to Crymmych-Arms, Pembrokeshire. Length, 16¼ miles. Capital, 37,000*l*. in 10*l*. shares and 12,500*l*. on loan. Great Western to provide a narrow gauge communication to Whitland, and to afford facilities.

The construction of the line was commenced in November last, and vigorous efforts are being made to open it for traffic in the course of the summer. The cost of the line, including land and preliminary expenses, will be about 2,600*l*. per mile.

No. of Directors—6; minimum, 3; quorum, 3 and 2. *Qualification*, 200*l*.

DIRECTORS:

Chairman—STEPHEN W. LEWIS, Esq., Regent Street, London.

David Davies, Esq., Llandinam, Montgomeryshire.
John Barrow, Esq., Ringwood, Chesterfield
Benjamin Evans, Esq., Cyaigill, Cardigan.
John Owen, Jun., Esq., Glogue Slate Quarries, Newcastle-Emlyn.
William Owen, Esq., Withybush, Haverfordwest.

OFFICERS.—Sec., Howell Davies, Carmarthen; Eng., J. W. Szlumper, C.E., Aberystwyth; Solicitors, J. H. and R. Tyas and Huntington, London.

Offices—123, Lammas Street, Carmarthen.

Extract from Bradshaw's 1871 Shareholders' Manual

Chapter Seven
In the Shadow of the Great Western: 1880–1883

By now a take-over by the GWR was generally expected, and most believed it would be sooner rather than later, not realising how long negotiations would take. In the meantime a growing English interest was evident in the Boardroom with the presence of John Griffith of Crowthorne, Berkshire, Stephen Lewis of Hornsey, and J.W. Bowen, QC, Auditor of the Great Western Railway. In 1880, however, the Whitland and Cardigan had nine Directors of whom only John Owen, and Benjamin Evans remained from the early years of the undertaking. The remainder also lived locally: they were Thomas Colby of Blaenffos (on the main road from Cardigan to Crymmych), Col Lewis of Boncath, Thomas Davies of Cardigan and Col Saurin of Orielton, Pembroke. The most notable omission from the Board now was David Davies. In view of his diverse commercial and political interests this was understandable even though as liberal MP for Cardigan Boroughs from 1874 he had good reason to be concerned for the railway.* Indeed he undoubtedly retained a keen interest, as was shown by his contribution to the negotiations between the company and the GWR and by his assistance in the settlement with Szlumper.

In fact the relationship between Davies and Szlumper is worth noting, and is a subject offering some scope for research. They were concerned with the W&TVR when their careers were still developing, but both were also involved in the P&TR, the Pontypridd, Caerphilly and Newport Railway, and the great Barry Railway and dock project of which David Davies was prime mover. In later life Szlumper (then Sir James Szlumper) played a part in the construction of both the Lynton and Barnstaple and the Vale of Rheidol narrow gauge railways. Meanwhile it must be noted that Howell Davies died in July 1880, and after the brief tenure of W.J. Morgan until December of that year, Mr G. Howell was appointed Company Secretary and General Manager.

By February 1881, the Board was able to tell shareholders that the Great Western Railway was ready to work the Whitland and Cardigan line for 70 per cent of the receipts in the first year, 65 per cent of the receipts in the second year, and, when traffic amounted to £9 per mile per week, 62½ per cent of the receipts. If the figures went over £10 per mile per week the charge was to be 60 per cent of the receipts, and if over £12 per mile per week it would be 55 per cent. These provisions were incorporated in a Bill then before Parliament, intended partly to govern relations between the original company and the Cardigan Extension Railway, and partly to facilitate the contemplated agreement with the GWR. The Whitland and Cardigan Railway Act, 1881, was duly passed by August, and included in its provisions authority for the construction of the railway on a new route between Boncath and Cilgerran. The deviation, which was the result of the new survey, was said to be '3 miles, 5 furlongs, 1 chain and 80 links' in length, with the sharpest curve of one furlong radius, and the steepest gradient 1 in 40. The

---

*He was not the first M.P. for Cardigan with an interest in railways. The earliest was Sir Humphrey Mackworth, who acquired leases in certain collieries near Neath in 1697 and constructed a waggonway there three-quarters of a mile long. The line survived until the pits shut down in 1809 or 1810.

deviation ran from 'Field No. 74 in the parish of Llanfihangel Pembedw to a junction with the (already) authorised line in Field No. 57 in the parish of Cilgerran.' This new line also passed through the parish of Manordivey.

One of the earliest excursions run on the W&CR was operated on 18th October, 1881. The trip was to mark the visit of the Prince of Wales to Swansea for the opening of the East Dock; intending passengers were advised that the train would start from Crymmych at 7.15 am. The journey to Whitland took an hour and 10 minutes and connected with the GWR excursion train at Whitland. As the return train did not depart from Swansea until 4 pm any travellers from Crymmych would have had a long day. The fares on the Whitland and Cardigan, though, were regarded as extremely cheap. A return excursion ticket from Crymmych to Whitland was 1s. 6d. and from Llanglydwen 10d. Soon after the company concluded that such fares were too generous. In December 1881, the Board decided to increase ordinary passenger fares to 3d./mile first class, 2d./mile second class and 1¼d./mile third class. The increases applied to all trains except the up and down mail trains, and came into force on 1st January, 1882. These rates were also applied when the railway to Cardigan opened in 1886.

In the summer of 1882 the task of getting construction of the Cardigan Extension under way had become urgent, not least because it was necessary to notify owners of the land required before the statutory time limit was reached on 1st August. Steps to raise the further capital required resulted in a local subscription raising £6,600. From the point of view of the Whitland and Cardigan Railway this was still hardly enough, but on the strength of it, and pending agreement with the GWR, the Directors decided unanimously to send the necessary notices to the landowners.

By now the deal with the Great Western seemed to be nearing a climax. On 9th and 10th August, the Board met at the Great Western Hotel, Paddington, for a Special Meeting, and toiled through what were clearly tedious negotiations. Throughout representatives of the GWR wanted local interests to put up more money, and the W&CR Directors resisted, being most reluctant to commit themselves any further than need be. Solicitors hurried to and fro between the parties and by the afternoon of 10th August the main issue was whether or not the Directors would pay a deposit on 429 Ordinary £10 shares, the additional amount the GW deemed necessary to finish the extension. The Directors decided that they would, but only as a subscription and without any further liability. Even then the final drafts of two Agreements between the companies (one dealing with working and one subsidiary) were incomplete, and the solicitors for each side continued to discuss the small print.

The half-yearly meeting held on 27th October 1882 was notable for the reported improvement in the financial condition of the company. Gross receipts for the half year were up by £227 19s. 3d. over the same period in 1881, and £305 5s. 2d. over the same period in 1880. References to the staff of the railway were many and frequent in the company Minutes at this time, and fascinating for their diversity. On the evening of 5th September, 1882, two drunken sailors assaulted guard Evans at Crymmych. Two weeks later they were fined 30s. and costs by the magistrate at Newport. Evidently guard

Evans was no angel himself, because at a Board meeting about four months later it was reported that he had insulted the Manager: the Board ordered Evans to apologize and gave a warning that if any similar charge was brought in the future he would be dismissed. In October 1882 the gangers and platelayers put in an application for wage increases, asserting that they did not receive the same rate as their counterparts on the Pembroke & Tenby Railway, but deserved parity. In addition engine driver J. Salmon, who received 2s. a week less than driver T. Davies, put in a claim for a comparable sum, pointing out that Davies had less work to do. With rough justice the Board decided that Davies' extra 2s. should be divided, making each man's wages the same! Perhaps it was a measure of some slight increase in prosperity that soon after, in February 1883, the wages of the station master at Crymmych were increased from 27s. 6d. to 30s. per week.

More meetings between representatives of the Whitland and Cardigan and the Great Western to thrash out the details of the agreements took place in December 1882, but negotiations did not draw to a close until 8th February, 1883. Copies of the agreements were laid before a meeting of the W&CR Board held on 23rd February, and it was decided to call a half-yearly meeting of shareholders on 28th February to signify the Directors' acceptance of the terms. This was duly done, the shareholders being informed that only one or two points in the subsidiary agreements were outstanding. At the same time it was reported that the railway's gross receipts were again up and the prospects were better.

The Extraordinary General Meeting of the shareholders held at the Guildhall, Cardigan, on 16th March, 1883, was attended by a large number of the shareholders including all those most active in the project and the Mayor of Cardigan in person. They were told that the GWR had sanctioned the agreements at a General Meeting held a short time before, and they approved unanimously the agreement for the 'working, maintenance and user' of the

A notable event: a photograph believed to be of the opening of the railway to Cardigan on 1st September, 1886. *D. Davies Collection*

Whitland and Taf Vale and the Cardigan Extension Railways. The meeting concluded in an air of satisfaction and renewed optimism, no doubt fortifying the Directors for their next meeting at the Great Western Hotel, Paddington on 24th April. On this occasion working plans for the extension were laid before the Board by the Engineer, and when the meeting resumed the next day the agreements sealed by the respective companies and exchanged were the Working Agreement, the Subsidiary Agreement, the Solicitors' Agreement and the Engineers' Agreement. At the same time on 25th April the contract with Messrs Appleby and Lawton, which was for a total value of £48,720, was also signed (together with two copies of the specification).

After many months of negotiation the Whitland and Cardigan was now certain to become part of the Paddington empire. At the heart of the agreements of 1883 was the scheme for the GW to take over the working of all train services as soon as the Cardigan Extension was open for traffic. Operation of the railway in the interim was thus on a caretaker basis and indeed, as already described, a sense of the management as being provisional was manifest at least as early as 1880. The evidence of the company's papers does not suggest that the management was much distressed by the take-over but rather that it and some of the shareholders may even have been relieved! In any event it can well be argued that the company brought its fate upon itself by pursuing the plan for the Cardigan extension. It was this ambition more than anything else which stretched the company's resources to the limit, and ultimately ensured that the assistance of the Great Western would have to be sought. The railway may have suffered from the GW's heavy charges, not to mention periods of poor receipts and rent charges on the land for the original line, but the company put the task of completing the line to Cardigan first, and it lost its independence in consequence.

The village of Glogue seen from the Quarries with the station (*middle right*).
Oakwood Collection

Chapter Eight
Construction and Reconstruction: 1883–1886

Construction of the Cardigan Extension began on 1st May, 1883 and went ahead rapidly. Two months later Walton reported that there were 330 men, 16 horses, one locomotive and a portable engine on the works, together with 270 tons of temporary rails, 3,000 temporary sleepers, one mile of wire fencing and 80 wagons. The earthworks were then built to a sufficient width across Cardigan marsh, and most of the heavy cuttings had been commenced. Clearly this progress owed something to the attempt to get construction under way in 1880, because Walton's report included the comment that 'a fresh road full gauge has been laid in the old workings in No. 1 cutting and a locomotive placed upon it.' Nevertheless at several places the contractors were not in possession of the land, because the company was continuing to have difficulties in negotiations for purchase. Acquisition was urgent because without it there was every prospect of new delays and complaints from the contractors. Furthermore the financial provision for the contractors was evidently incomplete: in July 1883, when Mr Appleby was entitled to £2,000 on account, the money was not produced immediately. Although none too happy at this hitch, the contractor allowed 10 days to elapse and eventually payment was sanctioned by some of those who knew they would become members of the Great Western and Whitland and Cardigan Joint Committee to be set up under Clause 3 of the Agreement of 8th February, 1883. In the circumstances the powerful backing of the GWR probably gave the contractor most comfort: the Agreements signed by the two companies enabled Directors appointed by the GWR to sit with Directors of the W&CR and exercise full powers in respect of the general business of the company.

On 2nd August, 1883, a Board meeting was held at the Great Western Hotel, Paddington, and the Great Western's three Directors for the Joint Committee were named. They were Mr Dillwyn, Mr Basset and Captain Gower. The W&CR's representatives were John Owen and Mr T. Davies (who had been a Director of the company for some time). Together they formed a committee to perform all acts relating to the affairs of the Cardigan company in connection with the construction of the CER, and the raising and expending of the necessary capital. Three members of the committee constituted a quorum. Meanwhile, because the company records were inadequate for an assessment of the works required to be carried out under the Agreement, Mr Walton was asked to make a new survey of the existing railway.

The Board protested on 29th February, 1884, at the amount of valuable time being lost by the fact that Mr Walton's survey had not gone ahead as anticipated. It was said that neither the Engineer nor his Assistant had been seen on the Extension works for a month, and so as concern mingled with indignation it was proposed that the Joint Committee should ask the GWR Engineer to inspect the works and report on progress. The contractors were now confident of having the line ready to carry coal and lime to Boncath by June 1884. Even so, as late as April 1884, some land for the Extension was still needed, and the prices were going up. A Mr Owen Davies wanted £400

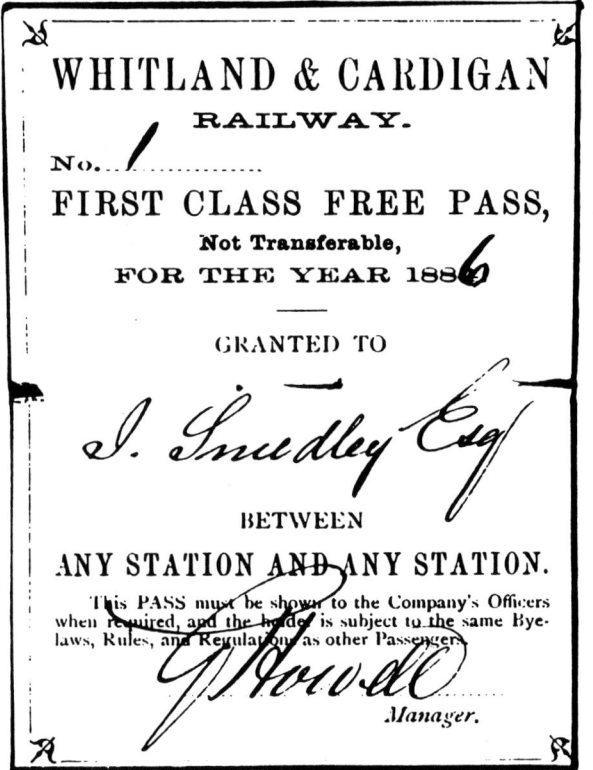

Isaac Smedley was the General Manager of the nearby Pembroke & Tenby Railway for many years.
Courtesy of Great Western Trust

for 3 roods, 13 perches of land and the provision of a cattle creep. The Board resolved to pay £350 and to make no cattle creep, and somehow the vendor was persuaded to agree. A Mr Sanders Davies then applied for siding accommodation at Boncath, Cilgerran and Cardigan, but he found the Board very reluctant to change its plans. Eventually, in September 1885, it was agreed to provide him with a siding at Boncath.

Mr Walton's first rough estimate for relaying the original line was no less than £26,000 — a figure which shook the Board somewhat because it was far beyond the £17,000 allowed in the agreements between the GWR and the W&CR. Mr Walton and Mr W.G. Owen (the Engineer representing the GWR) were asked to discuss it further. On 4th April, 1884, there was a meeting of the Board at Crymmych at which Mr Walton submitted the new surveys and gave verbal explanations as to the extent and cost of the alterations. He noted that under Articles 6 and 7 of the Agreement of 8th February, 1883 the GW was in the first instance to find £14,000 for relaying and repairing the old line, and a further sum of £3,000 if, in the opinion of the Engineers of the two companies the sum of £14,000 was insufficient for all the necessary works. In Walton's view the full amount of £17,000 was barely sufficient 'to relay the road with the heavy materials specified, and would leave no margin whatever for alterations to curves, re-arranging of stations, and further incidental expenses absolutely necessary to put the old line on a par with the Extension Railway.'

Clearly the condition of the railway was causing everyone anxiety, and not least the Engineer himself. On 21st April, apparently on his own initiative, he met Mr W.G. Owen at Paddington and agreed to communicate at once with the GW's representative in Wales, Mr Lloyd, preparatory to preparing a report and estimate for the Joint Committee. For a man who had shown little haste in making the surveys his change of mood and pace was remarkable: the report was dated 8th May, 1884! The reason was clear: Walton had come alive to the fact that the state of the line was deteriorating dangerously. He expressly said that he met W.G. Owen at Paddington with a view 'to relieving myself as quickly as possible, of whatever amount of responsibility might devolve upon me for being a party to keeping the railway open.' No doubt the presence of Mr Lloyd had contributed to his new found sense of anxiety. Sadly there is no record of their conversations at this time.

The Board received Mr Walton's full report at their meeting at Crymmych on 21st May, 1884, and after it had been approved by the Joint Committee. It made rather grim reading. He began by referring to 'delays which were doubtless unavoidable' in concluding the agreement with the GWR prior to February 1883. 'In the interval' he observed 'the Directors were compelled to accept the serious responsibility of working the line without the means for keeping it in efficient repair.' Even so the line had been carefully watched by the Inspector of permanent way and the small expenditure made was 'very judiciously laid out.' The cost of the works would now be at least £20,000, or £3,000 over the sum allowed in the Agreement with the GWR. The Engineer said he had carefully considered the question of flattening the curves below a radius of 12 chains, but had found that only a few could be altered without going outside the limits of the company's property and incurring serious expense in retaining walls and river bridges. The timber for the bridges required renewing throughout, and the fencing needed strengthening. In addition it was evident that it was only possible to lay down through loops at two of the stations (Llanfalteg and Crymmych) without buying more land.

Although so much attention was now being given to the state of the existing railway and the extension to Cardigan, the ordinary business of the company was continuing. The services required amendment from time to time: in anticipation of Good Friday, 11th April, 1884, Mr G. Howell produced a large poster to remind travellers that on that day only the mail trains would run, leaving Whitland at 6 am and Crymmych at 4.30 pm calling at all stations, and connecting with 'the GWR down and up mails'. A few weeks later he published another poster advising that in connection with the opening of Whitland Market Place market tickets at reduced fares would be issued on and from Friday, 23rd May for travel between Rhydowen and Whitland on the trains leaving Rhydowen at 8.28 am and 10.26 am. In the Taf Vale traffic was never very heavy, and the management had to seek custom whenever possible. Some of the schemes were most imaginative. On 23rd August, 1884, Mr Howell advertised the proposed sale six days later of cheap excursion tickets to Pembroke Dock and New Milford. The poster was boldly headed 'The Channel Fleet at Milford Haven'. On the day a wit added the words 'Did not come – did not run'. Sadly, this instance of Mr Howell's enterprise was not successful!

The permanent way from Crymmych to Boncath was completed in August 1884 and after some delay ballast was supplied from John Owen's tips. At this moment, though, the Chairman was not exactly happy about his financial arrangements with the company, and he said so. Even though he was to be paid £600 for stone used in improving the old line he claimed that the railway owed him £1,310 for ballast supplied between 1874 and 1884. He wished to ensure now that his siding at Glogue was relaid with the rest of the railway, although without any interference to his traffic. To underline the point he sought a formal resolution from the Board that the line from Glogue station to the quarries be deemed his property absolutely. This resolution was carried at the Board meeting held on 5th September, 1884. Some weeks earlier differences of opinion arose over the scale of charges for the carriage of contractor's traffic from Crymmych to Boncath. Some advocated high charges, and others (including Grierson of the GWR) disagreed, saying that high charges would be prejudicial to local trade. Meanwhile the contractors briefly engaged in a fiddle, receiving lime in their own name at Crymmych, and at their special rate, before passing it on to the Boncath Mercantile Company at a higher price. Not surprisingly the W&CR sought an explanation!

At the end of August the Board agreed to issue further debentures or debenture stock. The need for the additional capital was promptly emphasized by a couple of accidents on the existing line. On the morning of 3rd September, 1884, the engine and two coaches of the down mail ran off the line about a quarter of a mile south of Crymmych. There was little damage and, according to the Minutes, very little delay because 'the ballast engine was handy and worked the 8 am up train' from Crymmych. Quite how the up train so easily passed the derailed locomotive of the down train is not explained, but the track was blamed both then and on the morning of 30th October, when the down mail came off the line near Glogue as a result of a split rail. Once again the Board and the Engineer must have heaved a huge sigh of relief because the damage was minimal, and the delay to the mails a mere 20 minutes. Even so, such incidents were some incentive to get on with the task of relaying!

A half-yearly meeting of shareholders was held at Whitland on 27th February, 1885. Receipts for the half-year to 31st December, 1884 were up by £78 11s. 1d. over the corresponding half-year in 1883, and expenditure was down by £42 13s. 10d. It was reported that the original railway had been relaid as far as Login with 75 lb./yard steel rails, whilst on the extension all the permanent way had been laid but for 1¾ miles, mostly on the Bronhoel embankment near Cilgerran. The contractors had been carrying a lot of minerals over the line to Boncath, and this was partly responsible for the boom in traffic. Indeed the Directors were so encouraged that they recommended a dividend of 5 per cent on Preference shares for the six month period, but objections were raised in view of the company's indebtedness to the GWR totalling £3,586 19s. 1d. Following an adjournment of the meeting to 20th March it was resolved not to pay the dividend for this reason, even though the debt would be greatly reduced when the Great Western took over the rolling stock on the valuation then soon expected.

The month of August 1885 was eventful. The permanent way of the Cardigan Extension Railway was complete, and it seems that the company decided to celebrate this long awaited occasion in style. Accordingly a cheap railway excursion from Cardigan to Tenby and back was arranged for Monday, 10th August. Through carriages were provided, and the Volunteer Brass Band was in attendance. As the station buildings on the Extension were not ready for customers, the tickets were sold in advance through the agency of shopkeepers and others at Cardigan, Cilgerran, Boncath and Crymmych. The return fares from Cardigan and Cilgerran were: first class 5s., and third class 3s. 9d.; and from Boncath 4s. 9d. first class and 3s. 6d. third class. The train was not fast: it left Cardigan at 7 am, Cilgerran at 7.15 am, Boncath at 7.30 am and Crymmych at 8 am. The arrival time in Tenby was not specified, but at that pace it cannot have reached its destination before 10 am! The departure from Tenby was at 6 pm. This must have been the first passenger train in and out of Cardigan and of doubtful legality, because authority to operate a regular passenger service was not granted until over a year later. How the trip came to be organised thus remains something of a mystery, but on this occasion at least the W&CR was able to run its own train over the whole length of its line. For John Owen, who had struggled for so long to see the railway built, it must have been an immensely happy day.

Sadly his pleasure at this event quickly gave way to consternation over other matters. On 25th August, 1885 the 6.30 pm train from Whitland was involved in a fatal accident near Llanfalteg. Unfortunately exact details of the incidents are not recorded, but its seriousness lay in the fact that both enginemen were killed. A Board of Trade enquiry was held on 31st August,

1885, but the outcome was rather enigmatic. The Inspector simply decided that the crash did not occur from defects in the permanent way or in the rolling stock. Possibly the locomotive was at fault because an engine fitter gave evidence at the enquiry. The locomotive was certainly put out of action, because arrangements were speedily made to hire a replacement from the GWR.

If this incident was tragic, its significance for the company was less serious than a row over providing extra security against the advances over £17,000 given by the GWR under the Agreement of February 1883. John Owen doubted the legality of the measures proposed and tendered his resignation: he was soon restored to the Chair but on this issue his view was disregarded.

In September work on the Extension was almost complete, and the contractors had 'run their engines almost daily over the length of the line'. Accordingly opening to regular traffic was anticipated 'at an early day'. South of Crymmych relaying of the permanent way was also nearly complete. The only work still to be done was the doubling of the line at Llanglydwen, the building of station houses, completion of the fencing and renewal of signals and telegraphs. The signalling work was once again entrusted to Messrs Mackenzie and Holland of Worcester.

Two or three schemes for enlarging facilities on the W&CR were now under consideration. One proposal was for the construction of a siding to works at Cilgerran owned by the Director, Captain Gower. A larger scheme was for the extension of the line by railway or tramway to the quay on the Teifi at Cardigan. This notion, a reminder of the early Carmarthen and Cardigan Railway plan to build a line through the town to the quay, had several supporters on the Board.

By the middle of November the Cardigan Extension Railway was said to be nearly ready for inspection. However Cardigan yard was not finished, some ballasting was required between Crymmych and Boncath, and the coping stones had to be placed on several bridges. Appleby and Lawton complained that they had been waiting for two or three months for some materials and could not keep their men waiting longer. Their contract was practically complete, for the outstanding works could be done in seven or ten days, and in their view need not interfere with a Board of Trade inspection. The Board took note of these points, but was taken aback when in a letter dated 22nd December, 1885, the contractors asked for £17,786 for works carried out in excess of contract. On 2nd January, 1886, Manchester solicitors acting for Appleby and Lawton wrote demanding cash payment, and threatening the issue of a writ unless there was immediate payment of £1,000. The Board decided to send £1,000 at once, but not surprisingly in view of the size of the claim the argument did not die down. On 30th January the contractors wrote to the Company Secretary to say that they would run no traffic on the Extension after 14th February. In fact this was a threat they preferred not to fulfil, and so the dispute dragged on.

By the end of 1885 the take-over of W&C services by the GWR on the completion of the Cardigan Extension Railway was believed to be imminent. For this reason most of the shareholders in the local company tended to lose

A good view of Crymmych Arms station showing clearly the very acute curved platforms, c.1900.

R.E. Bowen Collection

interest, and indeed the half-yearly meeting arranged for 3rd March, 1886, had to be adjourned *sine die* because no shareholders turned up to form a quorum. Only a plan put forward by the GWR to close the stations at Login, Rhydowen and Glogue still aroused much concern. The Board fought for their retention, pointing out that local people did use them, and that the Directors had given undertakings about them when shareholders had paid for their shares. A note was received from Grierson saying that the receipts were too small and that if Login, Rhydowen and Glogue did not pay within a year after the GW took over operation, they would be closed.

A proposal for a Great Western engine shed at Whitland was pursued, and one suggestion made in order to solve the problem with a minimum of cost, was that negotiations should be conducted with the Pembroke and Tenby Railway with a view to enlarging their locomotive shed at Whitland. The W&CR did not object to the idea in itself, but some of the Directors still opposed incurring any expense on it even though the facility would be of benefit to the W&C line in the long run. John Owen in particular disliked the plan, and again he vacated the Chair rather than put Grierson's proposal before the Board when it met on 4th January, 1886. Col Lewis took over once again, and when the matter came to a vote four Directors voted for it and two against.

As it happened this meeting was the last at which John Owen actually occupied the Chair, and in June 1886, he died, aged 68. Although he had lived to enjoy the sight of the first trains from Cardigan, his last years seem to have been sad. In spite of all the work he had done in negotiating the Agreement with the GWR he appears to have found it hard to come to terms with the reality of the new relationship it created between the companies. He was buried in the graveyard adjoining the Congregational chapel at Llwynyrhwrdd, near Glogue, on a hillside overlooking the valley he loved and the railway he served so well. Ironically his death very nearly coincided with the end of W&CR working of the railway. If any man personified the enterprise it was John Owen: his departure at this moment was symbolic.

Llanglydwen station as seen on an early commercial postcard.   *Author's Collection*

Chapter Nine
The Great Western Takes Over: 1886–1890

At the time of John Owen's death the Whitland and Cardigan Railway Company was entering its final phase. At the Board meeting held on 11th June, 1886, Col Lewis was elected Chairman. Another Director, Mr James took over John Owen's seat on the Joint Committee. Notice had been given to the Board of Trade that the Cardigan Extension was ready for inspection. The Inspector, Col Rich, made his visit on 29th and 30th June, but in spite of a great rush to get the last jobs done many items were still outstanding. The station buildings had not been completed, a 3,000 gallon water tank had not been delivered, and work on the signals was unfinished. Inevitably, Col Rich postponed the opening of the line, but only for one calendar month from 6th July. In his report Col Rich included a request for bridge strengthening work to be completed, and the provision of sleeping accommodation at the crossing keepers' lodges. Mr Walton consulted the Board of Trade about the details, and managed to get the report's requirements reduced to a minimum. Of these the question of sleeping accommodation at crossing lodges seemed to be the most difficult, and on 23rd July a Whitland and Cardigan deputation went to the Board of Trade to give an undertaking to operate no night trains on the railway, and to shut level crossing gates at night in favour of road traffic. However the Board of Trade was insistent, and so steps were taken to attend to the lodges at Penclippen and Rhydowen at once. At Llanfalteg and Glogue it was agreed that lodges were not needed because local cottages could be rented. At Llanglydwen and Llanfyrnach, though, rooms were to be built over the stations: it is not clear how far this necessitated a change in plans for the stations then being built.

On 21st August Mr Howell, the Company Secretary, went to London and saw officials of both the Board of Trade and the GWR. The outcome was most encouraging. The Board of Trade said that no further inspection would be needed provided satisfactory replies could be given to each of Rich's points, and an undertaking given by the GWR to build the crossing lodges within a reasonable time. This the Great Western was ready to do, and it was also content to operate the railway from 1st September, 1886, provided an agreement securing their cash advance for the completion of the unfinished works was sealed by the W&CR. The agreement was duly sealed on 27th August and the GWR notified. Accordingly arrangements were made to open the Cardigan Extension Railway for traffic on Tuesday 31st August, 1886, and to hand it over to the GWR on the evening of the same day to enable them to begin working the next morning. The Minute on the matter concludes by mentioning that the Company Secretary would then take the books for audit before having one or two weeks holiday!

These arrangements evidently went ahead as planned, but it is not known what sort of service was operated on 31st August, 1886. Suffice to say that it was the second and last time that the W&CR operated public passenger trains over the Cardigan Extension. Presumably the GWR began working the line on 1st September, 1886, because that date was more convenient for administrative and book-keeping purposes. Certainly much more publicity has been given to the later date in references to the opening of the railway to

CARDIGAN BRANCH.

Single Line. worked by Train Staff and Ticket and Auxiliary Block Telegraph.

DOWN TRAINS. WEEK DAYS.

Mls.	Distances from Whitland	Stations	1 Passenger		2 Passenger (Saturdays only)		3 6.0 a.m. Goods ex Carmarthen Junction.		4 Market Train. B		5 Goods.		6 Passenger.		7 Passenger.	
			arr. A.M.	dep. A.M.	arr. A.M.	dep. A.M.	arr. A.M.	dep. A.M.	arr. A.M.	dep. A.M.	arr. A.M.	dep. A.M.	arr. A.M.	dep. P.M.	arr. P.M.	dep. P.M.
—	2	Whitland	...	6 0	...	...	...	6 40	...	8 10	...	10 0	...	12 0	...	6 30
2	3	Taf Vale Junction	6 5	6 9	...	...	8 6	8 11	8 17	8 23	10 6	10 11	12 5	12 6	6 38	6 48
5	3	Llanfallteg	6 18	6 21	...	...	8 16	8 22	8 32	8 40	10 16	10 26	12 12	12 15	6 47	6 51
8	3	Login	6 27	6 32	...	8 45	X8 45	X8 45	8 45	8 49	10 30	10 40	12 21	12 25	6 56	6 57
12	3	Rhydowen	6 39	6 44	...	9 0	8 53	...	8 54	8 58	...	X10 55	12 29	12 30	...	7 —
14	3	Llanfyrnach	6 50	6 53	9 11	9 15	...	...	9 4	9 9	10 55	11 15	12 37	12 42	...	7 14
16	3	Glogue	7 4	7 9	8 57	9 9	9 20	9 30	9 12	...	11 15	11 25	12 43	12 51	7 23	7 29
21	3	Crymmych Arms	7 19	7 20	9 11	9 15	9 30	X10 20	R R	Last Tues-day in each month.	11 25	11 45	12 51	X12 53	7 37	7 37
24	3	Boncath	...	...	...	...	10 40	...	...	...	11 45	12 12	...	1 5	...	7 49
27	3	Kilgerran	...	...	...	...	...	...	...	...	12 20	12 50	...	1 17	...	7 50
		Cardigan	7 30	...	9 25	...	R R	...	...	...	1 10	...	1 30	...	8 0	...

UP TRAINS. WEEK DAYS.

Mls.	Distances from Cardigan	Stations	1 Passenger		2 Empty Train. A (Saturdays only)		3 Passenger		4 Carmarthen Junction Goods. B B		5 Cattle. C		6 Goods. D		7 Passenger.	
			arr. A.M.	dep. A.M.	arr. A.M.	dep. A.M.	arr. A.M.	dep. A.M.	arr. P.M.	dep. P.M.	arr. P.M.	dep. P.M.	arr. P.M.	dep. P.M.	arr. P.M.	dep. P.M.
—	3	Cardigan	...	7 55	...	7 55	...	9 40	...	...	...	...	...	1 45	...	4 10
3	3	Kilgerran	8 6	8 8	8 17	8 18	9 50	9 51	...	11 40	...	...	1 57	2 0	4 20	4 31
6	3	Boncath	8 19	8 20	8 30	8 30	10 0	10 3	11 55	X12 55	Last day in each month.	3 0	2 25	2 40	4 31	4 33
13	3	Glogue	8 31	8 32	...	...	10 17	10 26	5 6	1 10	...	...	2 57	3 15	4 45	4 47
14	3	Rhydowen	...	...	...	...	10 30	10 31	...	C R	...	...	3 25	3 45	5 0	5 13
17	3	Llanfyrnach	8 43	8 44	...	...	10 39	10 39	1 35	1 40	3 35	...	3 41	4 15	5 13	5 21
21	3	Login	8 51	X8 52	...	...	10 43	X10 44	...	C R	...	4 20	4 25	4 30	5 21	5 30
23	3	Llanglydwen	...	...	...	...	10 52	11 1	2 13	C R	4 30	...	4 40	4 50	5 30	5 31
25	3	Taf Vale Junction	9 10	...	...	...	11 5	...	2 25	2 35	4 45	...	5 5	...	5 35	...
27	3	Whitland	...	...	...	...	11 10	...	...	...	...	...	...	...	5 40	...

A Also run on third Wednesday in each month.
B See note on page 6 respecting Crymmych monthly market.
C A Third Class Coach to be attached for Drovers.
D Two Third Class Coaches to be attached to this Train at Crymmych on last Tuesday in each month.

NO SUNDAY TRAINS.

On Good Fridays and Christmas Days No. 1 Down and No. 7 Up only run.

Form of Staff and Ticket.	Colour of Staff and Ticket.	Sections.	The Crossing Stations are—
Triangular	Red	Taf Vale Junction and Llanglydwen	Llanglydwen
Round	Yellow	Llanglydwen and Crymmych Arms	Crymmych Arms
Square	Blue	Crymmych Arms and Boncath	Boncath
Triangular ..	Red	Boncath and Cardigan	

Speed of Trains between Taf Vale Junction and Cardigan and vice versa.

Engine Drivers are forbidden under any circumstances to exceed the speed at which Ordinary and Special Trains are booked to run. Specials run without detailed times being fixed must in no case exceed a speed of 20 miles per hour.

Working timetable for the branch, May 1888

Cardigan, but then it appears that the GWR's reign was inaugurated with more ceremony. When the GW's first train arrived in Cardigan it was greeted by the Mayor and a brass band and a large crowd, including many local tradesmen. In addition 100 children were given a free ride on the line between Crymmych and Cardigan, and of these at least one, Herbert James of Pontygafael (near Rhydowen) lived to see the railway's last day in 1962.

Under the Agreement of 1883 the rolling stock of the Whitland and Cardigan was now handed over to the GWR, and the necessary valuation was made on 13th September. The total of £2,038 was accepted by the W&CR, although £1,300 was said still to be owing to the London and Provincial Bank on locomotive No. 3.

The few shareholders who turned up to a meeting in Cardigan on 22nd October were told that receipts and expenditure had gone down in the period to 30th June, 1886 in comparison with the same period in the previous year. The drop in passenger traffic was especially noticeable, but in contrast to 1885 the railway was now having to cope with the onset of an economic depression. Although the opening of the Cardigan Extension produced some eloquently-expressed hopes for the future, the realities of the situation were not so encouraging. Llanfyrnach lead mine and the Glogue quarries were doing good business, but the farmers were not. Set alongside the obvious importance of the former industries the significance of agriculture in the Taf Vale may be overlooked too easily. However the traffic in livestock and agricultural goods may fairly be called bread and butter business for the line: if it had not been available in quantity in later years when the main industries failed, the railway would surely have closed much sooner than it did.

The pace of company business slowed considerably. Various debts were settled and by May 1887 it was reported that sums owing on locomotive No. 3 had been paid. In March 1887 Col Lewis declared his desire to resign the Chair on account of deafness, and Mr T. Davies took his place. Unfortunately he had hardly done so before he became seriously ill. Captain Gower took over for a number of meetings before a new Director, Mr A. Young of London was appointed Deputy Chairman and then Chairman. It was a sign of the times, for Mr Young had been involved in negotiations prior to the 1883 Agreement on behalf of the GWR. By now the complete take-over of the W&CR was anticipated, and shareholders lost interest. A half-yearly general meeting held on 16th March, 1888 was adjourned to 22nd June, and made special provision for the creation and issue of some new Preference shares and debenture stock for the general purposes of the company's undertakings.

On 22nd June, 1888, no shareholders turned up for the adjourned half-yearly meeting, and it had to be adjourned again. In fact there was little to discuss, because most business was still deferred. Eventually the half-yearly meeting was adjourned four times, to 15th June, 1889, before the Chairman decided to forget it, and adjourned it *sine die*. Although the Whitland and Cardigan had representatives on the Joint Committee, the GW was the real power in the land. Hence, the lack of activity by W&C Directors is scarcely to be wondered at.

By 1890 Great Western services on the W&CR had settled into a pattern of four passenger trains a day each way between Whitland and Cardigan. One extra train ran on Saturdays at 8.25 am from Crymmych to Cardigan, and on the last Tuesday in each month there was an additional service at 7.55 am from Whitland to Crymmych for the agricultural fair. It returned from Crymmych at 2.50 pm. A service of two coaches daily was still being run between Crymmych and Newport.

Arrangements were now in hand for the settlement of all outstanding claims prior to winding up the company. This soon became a matter of persuading the GWR to settle on the company's behalf, although negotiations for this purpose were somewhat delayed by Sir Daniel Gooch's death in October 1889. By 1890 the Great Western was ready to take over completely and a special General meeting of shareholders held at the Guildhall, Cardigan on 19th May, 1890, provides the final entry in the Minute Book of the Whitland and Cardigan Railway. The meeting was in effect a Wharncliffe meeting to approve the relevant clauses in a GWR private Parliamentary Bill (inter alia) to take over the railway. The company's Solicitor read out the proposed Agreement and explained the appropriate clauses. The Chairman set out the financial position of the company, and admitted that the results of working the line over the previous two years had shown clearly 'how hopeless the condition of the company was.' A resolution approving the relevant part of the Great Western's Bill was carried.

The vesting of the undertakings of the W&CR in the GW was provided for by Section 47 of the Great Western Railway Act, 1890*, which also allowed for the appointment of a Liquidator for the local company. Mr Young the Chairman was made Liquidator; on 19th December, 1890, the balance of the purchase monies was paid to him by the GWR and he executed a conveyance of the W&CR's undertakings to the Great Western. The independent life of the railway thus quietly expired, although Mr Young still had to perform the burial. On 31st December, 1890, he wrote to shareholders from his office at 41 Coleman Street, London EC regarding the distribution of monies at the rate of £2 per Preference share and £1 per Ordinary share. In 1891 the job was done, and the W&CR became part of history.

* The Act was dated 4th August, 1890, although the W&CR was vested in the GWR with effect from 1st July, 1890.

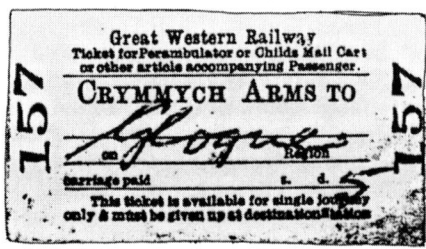

CARDIGAN BRANCH.

Single Line, worked by Train Staff and Ticket and Auxiliary Block Telegraph.
ON GOOD FRIDAYS AND CHRISTMAS DAYS, No. 1 DOWN AND No. 13 UP, ONLY RUN.

Form of Staff and Ticket.	Colour of Staff and Ticket.	Sections.	The Crossing Stations are—
Square	Blue	Taf Vale Junction and Llanfalteg	
Triangular	Red	Llanfalteg and Llanglydwen	Llanglydwen
Round	Yellow	Llanglydwen and Crymmych Arms	Crymmych Arms
Square	Blue	Crymmych Arms and Boncath	Boncath
Triangular	Red	Boncath and Cardigan	

SPEED OF TRAINS BETWEEN TAF VALE JUNCTION AND CARDIGAN AND VICE VERSA.

Engine Drivers are forbidden under any circumstances to exceed the speed at which Ordinary and Special Trains are booked to run. Specials run without detailed times being fixed must in no case exceed a speed of 20 miles per hour.

BRAKE POWER IN PASSENGER TRAINS BETWEEN WHITLAND AND CARDIGAN.

Maximum Load, 9 vehicles, and not to exceed 44 wheels in all. Rear Passenger vehicle to be a Brake, Guard to ride in it.

ASSISTANT ENGINES.

When an assistant Engine is run with a Goods, Mineral, Cattle, or Ballast Train between Taf Vale Junction and Cardigan it must be attached as follows :—

From	To	Position.
Whitland	Glogue	In Front.
Glogue	Crymmych Arms	At Rear.
Crymmych Arms	Cardigan	In Front.
Cardigan	Crymmych Arms	At Rear.
Crymmych Arms	Whitland	In Front.

WORKING OF GOODS AND CATTLE WAGONS BY PASSENGER TRAINS ON WHITLAND AND CARDIGAN BRANCH.

Vehicles not fitted with Vacuum Pipes attached to the Trains marked "Mixed" must be worked in strict accordance with Mr. BURLINSON's Circular No. 889, dated December 4th. 1893.

CRYMMYCH ARMS and BONCATH STATIONS.—During shunting operations at Crymmych Arms and Boncath Stations, the Engine must, in all cases, be attached to the Vehicles about to be moved, and a man must be on the ground to attend to the Brakes of the Vehicles and to detach the latter when they are placed in the Sidings. Whenever the Engine of a Passenger Train, either Up or Down, is about to be detached for any purpose, the hand-brake in the Guard's Van must be tightly screwed on to prevent the possibility of the Train running away.

CRYMMYCH MONTHLY MARKET.—The Station Inspector at Crymmych to arrange for Lime, Coal, and other wagons, to be worked to Glogue by the 10.50 a.m. Goods ex Boncath on the previous day, to remain there until Wednesday, so that there may be room for the Cattle to be dealt with expeditiously.

Loaded Trucks of Coal and Lime for Crymmych on Down Trains on Monday and Tuesday, to be put off at Glogue, to go forward on Wednesday morning.

The load for a Cattle Train worked by one Engine from Crymmych to Whitland will be 22 Trucks of Cattle, 1 G. B. Van, and a Third Class Coach for the conveyance of Drovers may be added when necessary.

The Station Masters at Whitland and Cardigan must arrange to strengthen the Ordinary Trains as necessary. The Whitland Tickets of Down Mails on this date must be collected at St. Clears, and the Crymmych Tickets of Down Branch Mail must be collected at Glogue.

BONCATH.—During shunting operations at Boncath Station, the Engine must, in all cases, be attached to the vehicles about to be moved, and a man must be on the ground to attend to the Brakes of the Vehicles, and to detach the latter when they are placed in the Sidings.

MAXIMUM LOADS OF GOODS TRAINS—CARDIGAN BRANCH.

FROM	TO	TANK ENGINE.				SMALL TANK ENGINE.			
		A Ordinary Goods.	A Mixed Goods and Empties.	C Coal.	C Empties.	A Ordinary Goods.	A Mixed Goods and Empties.	C Coal.	C Empties.
Whitland	Crymmych	14	15	9	18	10	12	7	14
Crymmych	Cardigan	18	20	12	24	15	17	10	20
Cardigan	Crymmych	15	17	10	20	12	13	8	16
Crymmych	Whitland	22	27	17	34	20	25	15	

Notes.—A Coal, Mineral, Tin, Grain, Stone, Timber, or other Heavy Mileage Traffic not included.
C Traffic shown under Note A included.

CARDIGAN BRANCH.

List of Gradients Steeper than 1 in 200.

From	To	Gradient. 1 in	Fall or Rise
Taf Vale Junction	Crymmych Arms	55	Rise
Crymmych Arms	Boncath	60	Fall
Boncath	Cardigan	40	Fall

GWR Service timetable and Regulations for October 1894

CARDIGAN BRANCH.

Down Trains. Week Days. No Sunday Trains.

M.C.	Distances from Whitland.	Station	1 A Passenger arr. A.M.	dep. A.M.	2 D Goods. RR arr. A.M.	dep. A.M.	D Goods. RR arr. A.M.	dep. A.M.	D Goods. RR arr. A.M.	dep. A.M.	D 7.0 a.m. Goods ex Cm'then Jc. L arr. A.M.	dep. A.M.	6 A Mixed Passenger. arr. A.M.	dep. A.M.	D Goods. N arr. P.M.	dep. P.M.	D Goods. N arr. P.M.	dep. P.M.	9 A Mixed Passenger. arr. P.M.	dep. P.M.	10 A Passenger. arr. P.M.	dep. P.M.	11 A Light Engine. dep. P.M.	12	13
—	—	Whitland		CS 6 0		CS 6 50		...		...		CS 7 40		10 15		CS 11 30		CS		CS 3 25		CS 6 15	7 30	...
2	1	Inf Vale Junc.	6 9	6 10	CS	...		...	8 11	8 15		...	10 20	10 22	12 26	12 31		...	3 34	3 35	6 24	6 25	7 3½	...	...
3	52	Llanfallteg	6 18	6 19	CS	...		...		...		...	10 33	10 34	12 41	12 43		...	3 43	3 44	6 33	6 34	7 40	...	...
8	0	Login	6 27	6 28	7 21	7 25		...	8 35 X	8 42		9 0	10 42X	10 46	12 55	1 0		...	3 52 X	3 53	6 42 X	6 43	7 47	...	...
10	20	Llanglydwen	6 32	6 33		...		...		...		...	10 50	10 51	1 5	1 10		...	3 57	3 58	6 47	6 48	...	...	...
12	64	Rhydowen	6 40	6 41		...	H	...		9 0		9 5	10 58	10 59	1 20	1 25		...	4 5	4 6	6 55	6 56	...	...	...
14	11	Glogue	6 45	6 46	7 45	7 55		9X15	8 35 X	8 45		9 5	11 3	11 6	1 30	1 35		...	4 10	4 13	7 2	7 3	...	...	...
16	31	Crymmych Arms	6 57	6 58	8 10X	...		9 25	9 25 X	...		9 35	11 15	11 17	1 50 X	1 59 34		...	4 22	4 23	7 12	7 13	...	...	...
20	72	Boncath	7 9	7 10		...		...		9 55		...	11 28	11 30	2 40	2 43X		...	4 34 X	4 36	7 24	7 25	...	...	...
24	33	Kilgerran	7 20	7 21		...		...		...		...	11 40	11 41	2 55	3 5		...	4 45	4 46	7 35	7 36	...	...	...
27	39	Cardigan	7 30			...		...		K		Last Tuesday in each month	11 50		3 15			...	4 55		7 45		...	...	...

G 6.50 a.m. RR Goods, Whitland to Crymmych. To run on last Wednesday in month and on other dates when required. Staff Stations must be advised at what time it will return from Crymmych or Boncath.

H 9.0 a.m. Goods, Glogue to Crymmych. To run on last Wednesday in month to take to Crymmych Trucks kept back and removed, to free Crymmych Yard for Cattle loading.

K 8.0 a.m. RR Goods, Whitland to Boncath. This will not run on the dates when No. 6 is running.

L 7.0 a.m. Goods Carmarthen Junction to Crymmych. To run on last Tuesday in month, and take Cattle Wagons for Crymmych Monthly Market. Two Guards who are to assist in the loading of Cattle at Crymmych, to be sent with the Train from Carmarthen Junction.

N 11.30 a.m. Goods, Whitland to Cardigan. No. 8 Down, will run in three times on last Tuesday in month, and must not take Trucks for Stations short of Crymmych. Crymmych Trucks to be put off at Glogue unless specially ordered beyond. S. T. No. 30.

CARDIGAN BRANCH.

Week Days.   No Sunday Trains.

Up Trains.

Distances from Cardigan	Stations	1 A Light Engn. RR dep. A.M.	2 A Light Engn. RR dep. A.M.	3 A Mixed Passenger. arr. A.M.	3 A Mixed Passenger. dep. A.M.	4 D Goods. RR arr. A.M.	4 D Goods. RR dep. A.M.	5 D Goods. RR arr. A.M.	5 D Goods. RR dep. A.M.	6 A Mixed Passenger. arr. A.M.	6 A Mixed Passenger. dep. A.M.	7 D Goods. RR arr. A.M.	7 D Goods. RR dep. A.M.	8 B Cattle. RR arr. P.M.	8 B Cattle. RR dep. P.M.	9 A Light Engine. dep. P.M.	10 D Goods and Cattle. arr. P.M.	10 D Goods and Cattle. dep. P.M.	11 B Cattle. W arr. P.M.	11 B Cattle. W dep. P.M.	12 D Goods. V arr. P.M.	12 D Goods. V dep. P.M.	13 A Passenger. arr. P.M.	13 A Passenger. dep. P.M.	14 A Passenger. arr. P.M.	14 A Passenger. dep. P.M.
—	Cardigan	…	…	…	7 40	…	…	…	B	…	9 40	…	…	…	…	…	…	V 12 30	…	Last Tues-day in each month	…	12 50	…	4 10	…	5 35
3	Kilgerran	…	…	7 49	7 50	…	…	—	—	9 49	9 50	…	…	…	…	…	…	…	…	…	1 30	1 45	4 19	4 20	5 41	5 42
6	Boncath	…	…	8 2	8 3	…	…	—	—	10 2	10 10	…	…	…	…	…	1 0	1 10	…	…	2 2x	2 50	4 32x	4 33	5 57	5 58
11	Crymmych Arms	…	…	8 15	8 16	…	Q	—	X 9 15	10 15	10 16	…	5 11 25	U	Last Tues-day in each month	…	1 27	2 10	…	2 30	3 0	3 10	…	4 46	6 19	6 20
13	Glogue	…	…	8 21	8 22	…	…	9 25	9 35	10 21	10 27	11	T	OR	…	…	…	…	…	…	3 16	3 20	…	…	6 26	6 27
14	Llanfyrnach	…	…	8 29	8 30	…	…	—	—	10 31	10 32	…	OR	…	…	…	…	…	…	…	3 30	3 35	…	5 7	6 30	6 31
17	Rhydowen	…	…	8 37	8 38	…	…	—	—	10 39	10 40	…	OR	…	…	…	…	2 15	2 54	…	3 41x	3 55	5 9	5 10	6 35	6 36
18	Llanglydwen	…	P	8 42x	8 43	…	…	—	9 55	10 44x	10 45	11 55	OR	…	…	2 15	…	…	—	—	4 5	4 10	5 11	5 15	6 40	X 6 44
23	Login	…	O	8 50	8 51	…	…	—	10 15	10 52	10 53	—	OR	1 25	…	…	…	—	—	—	—	4 20	4 30	5 22	5 23	6 51	6 52
25	Taf Vale Junc.	6½	7 H	8 58	8 59	…	…	—	10x24	—	0 11	—	12 15	1 44	1 54	2 20	2 35	…	—	—	C/S	C/S	C/S	C/S	6 59	7 1
28	Whitland	6¼	7 3½	9 8	…	N 30	…	10 30	—	11 0	C/S	12 30	12x24	2 14	—	2 30	3 1	—	C/S	3 1	C/S	4 45	—	5 40	—	7 10	—

O   6.10 a.m. Light Engine. This runs when 6.50 a.m. conditional is required.
P   7.10 a.m. Light Engine. This runs when 8.0 a.m. conditional is required.
Q   8.30 a.m. RR Goods Crymmych to Glogue. To run on last Wednesday in month, and on other dates when required.
B   9.15 a.m. Goods, Crymmych to Whitland. To be worked by Engine, Guard, and Van arriving at 8.10 a.m. To convey to Glogue (when run on last Tuesday in month) any Trucks in the way of the Cattle Loading that may have been left over from Monday. This trip will not run where 1.0 p.m. Crymmych to Whitland is required.
T   10.50 a.m. RR Goods Boncath to Whitland. This will run on days when 8.0 a.m. RR Goods ex Whitland is run, also when 6.50 a.m. RR Goods ex Whitland is extended to Boncath.
U   1.0 p.m. Cattle Train Crymmych to Whitland. This will run on last Tuesday in month when the 6.50 a.m. ex Whitland is run on that date and when the Engine and men do not return from Crymmych at 9.15 a.m.
V   12.30 p.m. Goods, Cardigan to Whitland. No. 12 Up will run in these times on last Tuesday in month and must not take on Trucks at Cardigan except for Boncath, and one through Station Truck. To take Cattle, Crymmych to Whitland.
W   2.25 p.m. Cattle, Crymmych to Carmarthen Junction. To take Cattle and to be worked by Carmarthen Junction Engine and Van arriving at 9.15 a.m., and take on from Whitland the Cattle brought up by previous Trains.

Two interesting views of Whitland station before rebuilding.
Top: R.E. Bowen Collection; Below Author's Collection

Chapter Ten
The Route Described

Little is known about the layout and physical appearance of the original Whitland and Taf Vale Railway, the only information available being Col Rich's Report to the Board of Trade in 1875. Stations were provided at Llanfalteg, Login, Llanglydwen, Rhydowen and Crymmych, but Col Rich did not specify which of these were passing places. There can be little doubt that loops were laid in at Llanfalteg and Llanfyrnach as well as at the terminus at Crymmych, but it is believed that Llanglydwen was not given a passing loop until the 1880s. Glogue was provided with a platform at an early date, although a long quarry siding was laid in from the outset. In spite of Col Rich's recommendation that crossing places should have a second platform it appears that none were constructed before the original line was rebuilt in 1884–1886. For the first 10 or 12 years of the Whitland and Taf Vale the station buildings consisted of simple wooden sheds, each with a urinal. At Crymmych, though, where there was a refreshment room and other accommodation the buildings must have been larger.

The papers of the Whitland and Cardigan Railway, which often refer to amended plans for the construction or re-construction of stations and crossing lodges, do not make it exactly obvious what work was carried out between 1885 and 1887. In December 1885 mention was made of the need for permanent stations at Llanglydwen, Rhydowen and Glogue, but a few months later (afer the row about the possible closure of Login, Rhydowen and Glogue) the construction of permanent stations at Llanfalteg, Llanglydwen and Llanfyrnach was authorised. Crymmych was evidently re-built and enlarged in 1887, at which time the refreshment room was closed. As eventually constructed the main buildings at Login, Llanglydwen, Llanfyrnach and Crymmych were of similar style, whilst the smaller stone building at Llanfalteg was similar to those at Boncath and Kilgerran on the Cardigan Extension. Large stone station houses also stood near the railway at Rhydowen and Glogue, although the platform buildings were wooden and were probably those erected by Mr D. Rees of Whitland in 1886.

After the opening of the Pembroke and Tenby and Whitland and Taf Vale Railways the station at Whitland had four platform faces. Two of these served the main line, one served a loop round the down island platform and the other a bay behind the up platform, access to which was from the west. The main station buildings were on the up side and nearby, close to the bay platform, there was a goods shed and a few sidings. All these changed little until British Railways' days when the station was extensively modernised. In addition, in the 1960s the down loop was disconnected and became a bay for Pembroke Dock trains. On the down side, too, there was a small goods yard originally constructed for the use of the Pembroke and Tenby Railway, and for the exchange of traffic between that company and the GWR before the Great Western took over the working of the P&T in 1896. A short distance west of Whitland station the locomotive shed stood until the mid-1960s.

Passenger trains from Cardigan ran into either the bay or the up main platform at Whitland, but trains departing for Cardigan customarily shared the outer face of the down island platform with P&T line trains. The first 2

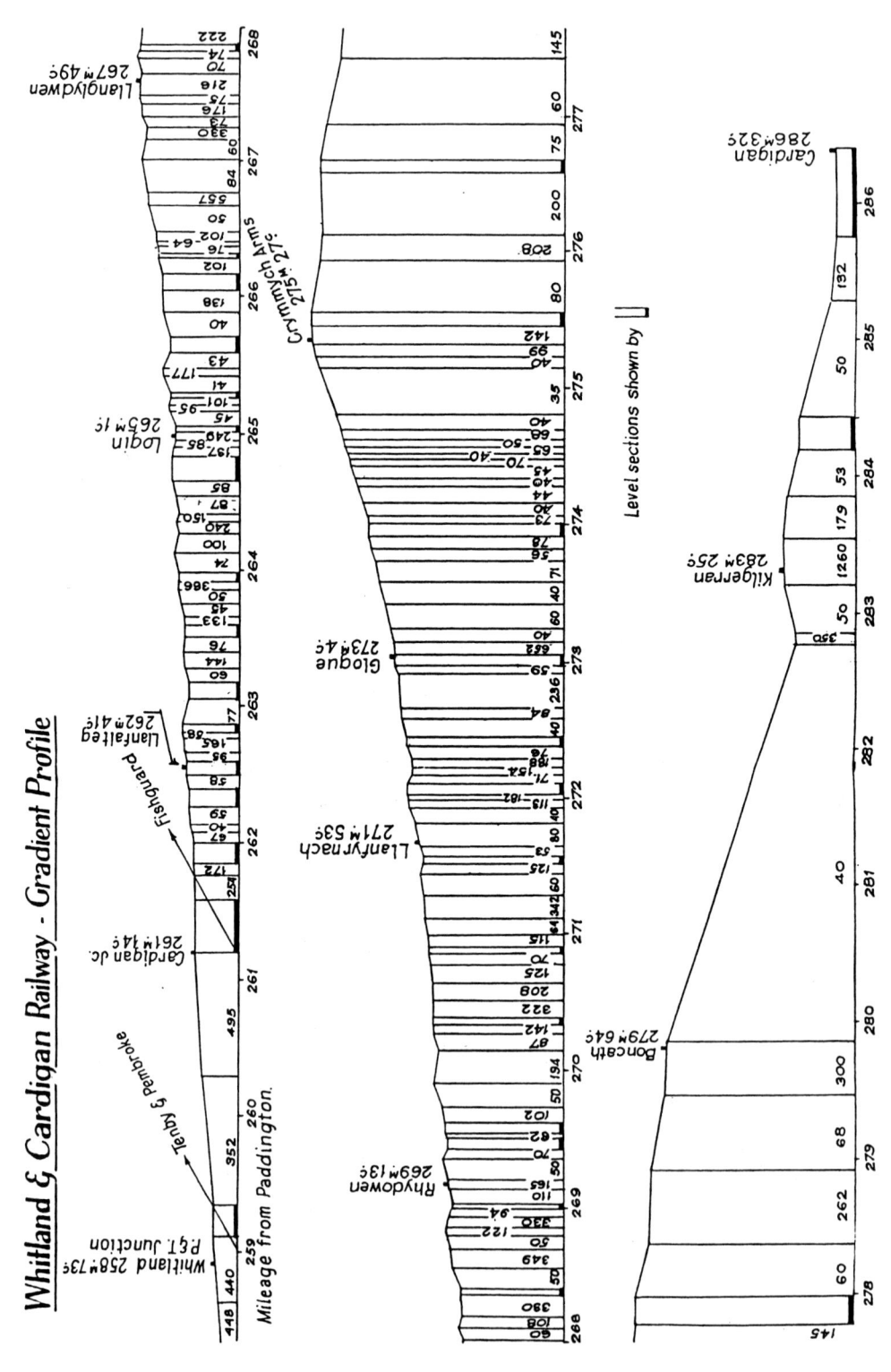

A '16XX' class, 0–6–0PT No. 1628 on 6.20 pm branch line train to Cardigan seen here at Whitland on 12th September, 1952.   *H.C. Casserley*

'45XX' class, 2–6–2T No. 5549 on the 4.00 pm train to Cardigan at the rebuilt Whitland station on 21st August, 1961.   *E. Wilmhurst*

Whitland shed on 22nd November, 1938 with No. 7318 on the turntable road into the shed. Note the coaling road on the right. *British Rail*

An earlier view of Whitland shed, c.1925. *British Rail*

A derelict view of Llanfalteg station looking north, 16th August, 1963.   *Author*

Llanfalteg station and ground frame hut looking south.   *Lens of Sutton*

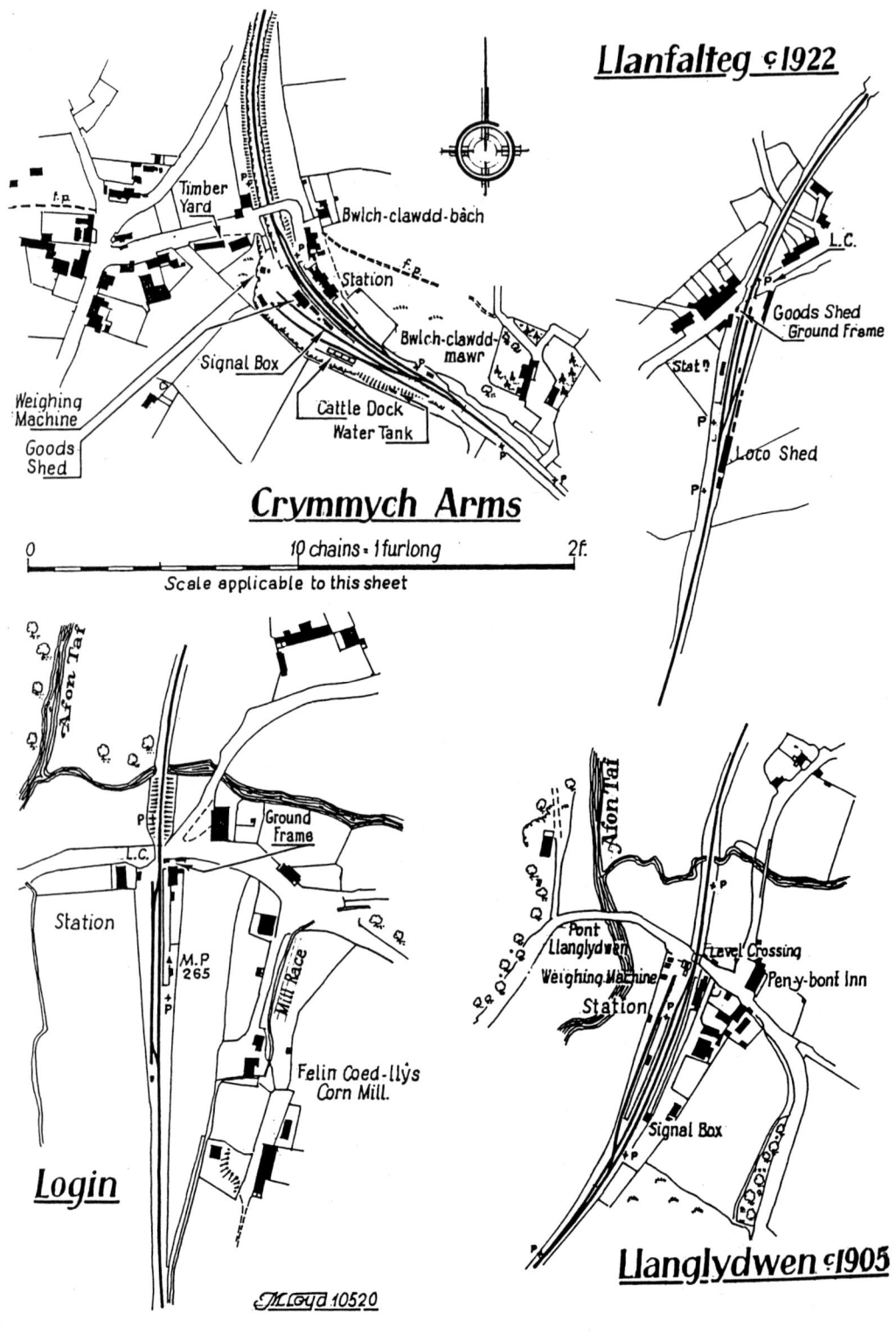

Login station, a view looking north showing the substantial station buildings for the size of the station.
Lens of Sutton

Login station, looking north from the level crossing.
Lens of Sutton

miles 21 chains of the route was along the main line to Cardigan Junction (originally Taf Vale Junction). Here the signal box, opening in 1873 and closed in 1964, was whitewashed, pebble-dashed and austerely domestic in appearance, being built entirely in stone or brick. The window overlooking the tracks was a modest rectangle with two uprights in the window frame. The nameboard 'Cardigan Junction' was located directly under it. The door was on the east side of the box, with another window, and the pitched roof was surmounted by a single chimney. A gaslight was situated outside.

The branch turned north from the junction and became a single track at once. A run of just over a mile brought the railway to Llanfalteg (3 miles 48 chains from Whitland). In the early years of the line, of course, this place had some importance. Until the re-construction of the mid-1880s the layout consisted of a loop, with a siding parallel to it to serve the goods shed, and a further siding for the locomotive shed and for coal traffic. In its heyday the locomotive shed had a forge for day to day repairs, but it was not big enough to be able to undertake major overhauls. After the Great Western took over the W&CR the shed at Whitland assumed most of the responsibilities of Llanfalteg shed, and gradually the latter fell into disuse. For a while it was occupied by Mr J. Williams' carpenter's shop, but this ceased and decay set in until eventually the shed fell down in about 1939.

At closure in 1962 the station building and the wooden ground frame box were intact, and a dilapidated iron goods shed still stood by the level crossing. The layout, however, was reduced: the loop had been replaced by a siding, and although the siding to the goods shed remained the rest of the trackwork had long gone. A length of rusting cable in the undergrowth provided the only evidence of the practice at Llanfalteg of cable-shunting. The site was cramped and inconvenient, and for many years the most effective way of moving wagons in and out of the sidings was by a cable linking them to a locomotive on a parallel track.

North of Llanfalteg the valley of the Taf begins to narrow, and the hillsides become steeper. Keeping to the east of the river the railway ran past Penclippen level crossing and its wooden crossing keeper's hut. For quite a number of years the crossing keeper was a woman, and there is a story that on one occasion she got her hands trapped under the frame of the window when she was trying to open it. Eventually she was released when the crew of a train halted at the signal came to investigate! With frequently changing gradients the railway continued to Login (6 miles). Here a short platform was dignified by the large station building serving the tiny hamlet perched on the hillside just across the river. The goods loop was protected by a ground frame at each end, that at the south end being just a single lever unlocked by the Cardigan Junction–Llanglydwen electric tablet. The ground frame at the north end, however, also controlled the level crossing, and it was housed in a wooden hut of typical Great Western design.

Between Login and Llanglydwen the gradients continued to change often as the track followed the lie of the land; the steepest grade on this section was 1 in 40. About half a mile north of Login was the tightest curve on the railway: it was short but built to a mere 8 chains radius. Llanglydwen station (8 miles 56 chains), the end of the first single line section, had up and down

Llanglydwen station with GWR 0–6–0PT No. 1637 ready to depart on a down train for Cardigan, 8th July, 1958.
R.M. Casserley

GWR 2–6–2T No. 4550 enters Llanglydwen station with the 5.45 pm train from Cardigan on the same day. Note the similar style station building to Login.
R.M. Casserley

Rhydowen station as seen from the rear of a down train for Cardigan on 8th July, 1958.
R.M. Casserley

Rhydowen station, a view looking north towards the level crossing.   *Lens of Sutton*

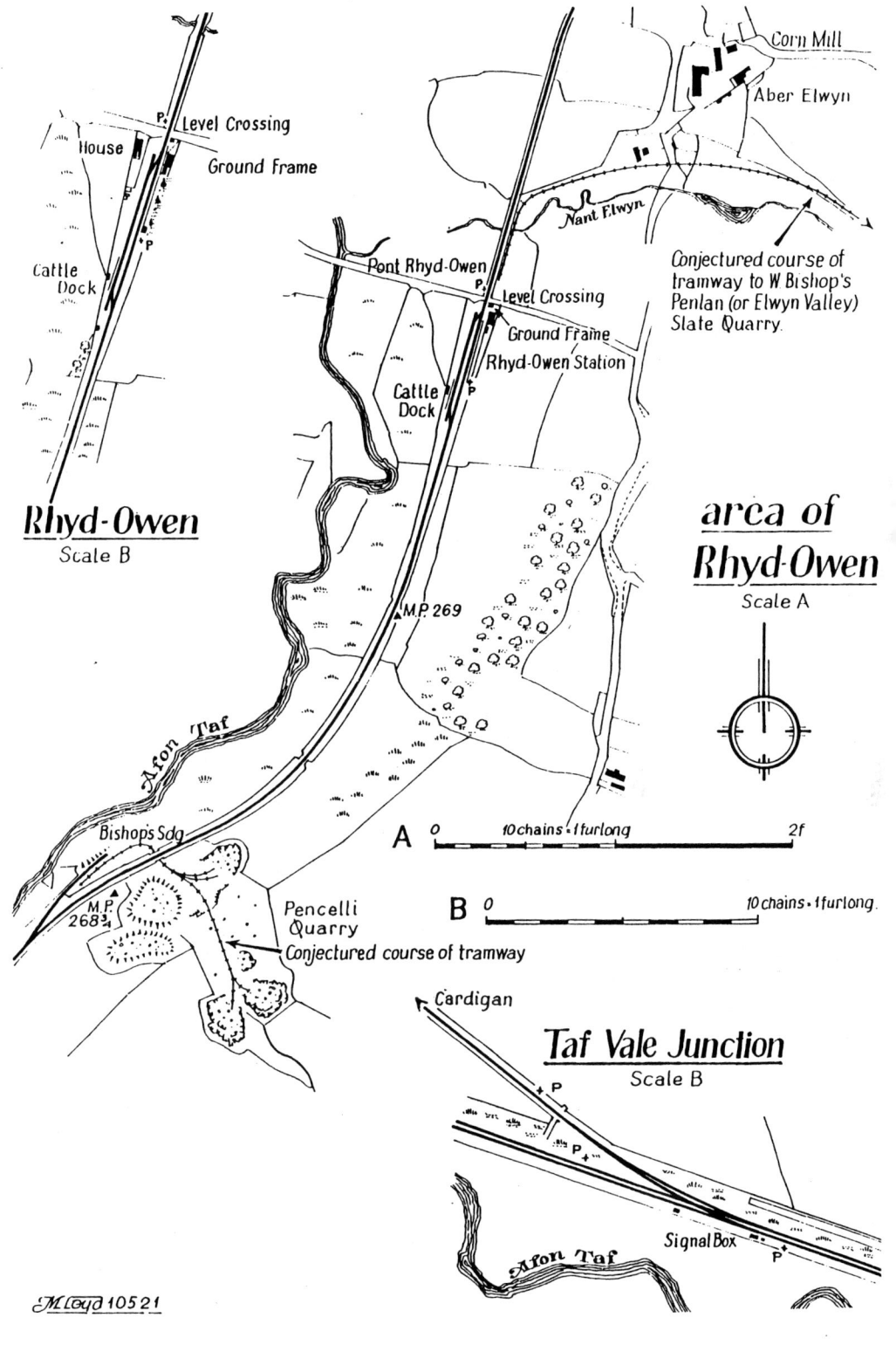

Llanfyrnach station and level crossing photographed in about 1920 looking towards the goods yard spur and cattle dock. *J.E. Davies*

Llanfyrnach station, a view looking south, 8th July, 1958. *R.M. Casserley*

The north end of Llanfyrnach station, showing goods siding and cattle dock.
Lens of Sutton

This view take befor World War I shows that the railway and the shop were the 'heart of life' in Glogue village.
R.E. Bowen Collection

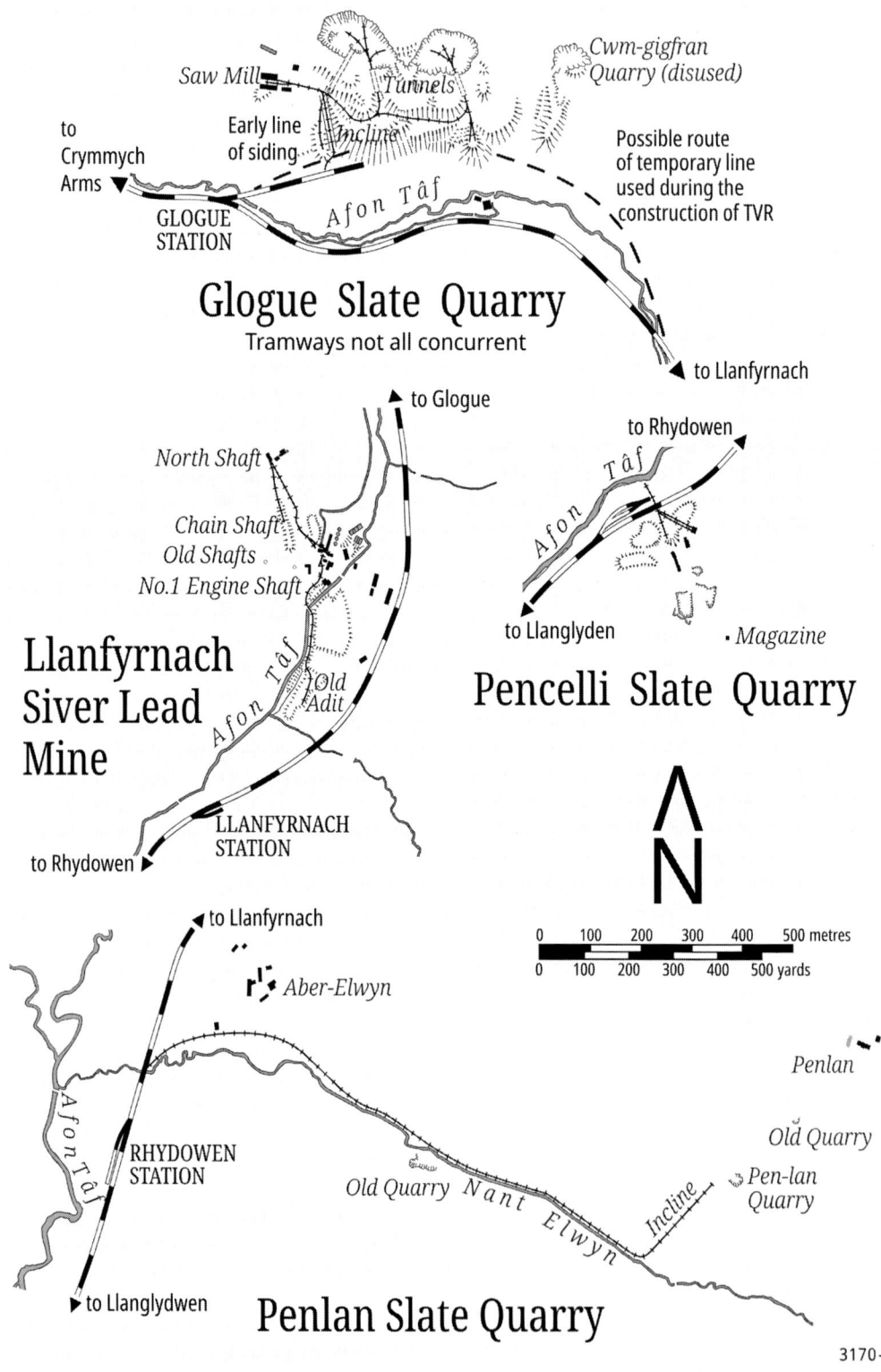

Glogue quarry seen from Glogue station. The stub of the former quarry siding is to the right.
D.G. Rogers

Ruined buildings at the Llanfyrnach silver-lead mine, as seen from the 'Cardi Bach' train, summer 1962.
D.G. Rogers

Glogue station and level crossing looking towards the view as seen on the previous page.
Lens of Sutton

A further view of Glogue station, view looking north.
R.M. Casserley

platforms and a coal siding. In accordance with usual practice on the branch, probably derived from independent days on the railway, the tablet instruments were kept in the station buildings. The Great Western style wooden signal box only enclosed a lever frame. For many years the evening passenger trains crossed at Llanglydwen during opening hours at the adjacent pub. Often one train would come in with some minutes to spare before the arrival of the other, and in anticipation of a short wait the locomotive of the first train would frequently approach Llanglydwen hooting furiously. This was a signal to the publican to pull pints for the crew's refreshment!

North of Llanglydwen the lineside was not so heavily wooded as on the lower portion from Login to Llanglydwen. However the railway remained close to the river, now a rather rocky and turbulent stream. About a mile and a quarter beyond Llanglydwen the line passed the site of Mr Bishop's short-lived siding for Pencelli quarry traffic before coming to Rhydowen (10 miles 20 chains). The undistinguished wooden station buildings were augmented by a goods loop, a ground frame and a level crossing. Latterly there was little sign of the connection made north of the station with the Penlan quarry tramway, although like the Pencelli tramway it had a very brief existence.

From Cardigan Junction to Rhydowen the railway ran inside the boundary of Carmarthenshire, but on leaving Rhydowen the line crossed the river Taf for the first time and passed into Pembrokeshire. The stream was crossed again during the climb (on gradients as steep as 1 in 50) up to Llanfyrnach (12 miles 60 chains). The level crossing was situated at the south end of this station, and the layout was unusual in that the goods loop was placed north of the station platform. In view of the extensive agricultural and coal traffic handled here the siding accommodation never seemed adequate. However in the early years of the railway, when the Llanfyrnach lead mine was in production, the facilities may have been better.

In the 20th century tips and other evidence of the mining industry remained on the left of the line as it continued to climb towards Glogue. The valley closed in here and the shrunken stream of the Taf re-appeared in marshy ground on the east side of the route before the bare, grey spoil heaps of the Glogue quarries came into view beyond. Glogue (14 miles 11 chains) was the approximate half way point once the railway reached Cardigan, and after the long haul up the Taf vale it was also the place where locomotives replenished their water tanks. In fact both up and down trains took water here, a procedure which entailed a halt of several minutes. At the north end of the platform the Glogue quarry branch joined the line, and because it faced Cardigan all traffic to and from it was worked via Crymmych Arms. In the last twenty-five years of the railway, at least, this branch was cut back to a short siding.

Beyond Glogue the hills became bleaker and the gradients worsened until just before Crymmych there was a 500 yd stretch at 1 in 35. Train crews undoubtedly entered Crymmych Arms with a great sense of relief! The

A good general view of Crymmych Arms station photographed in about 1900.
R.E. Bowen Collection

No. 4550 '45XX' class with the 6.22 pm southbound train arives at Crymmych Arms 31st July, 1959. *M. Francis*

A GWR '16XX' class No. 1637 passing a goods train at Crymmych Arms station on 8th July, 1958.
R.M. Casserley

The gentle curve of Crymmych Arms station, seen here looking north in 1960.
Oakwood Collection

A GWR '45XX' class 2–6–2T No. 4550 pauses at Crymmych Arms with an up train on 8th July, 1958. *H.C. Casserley*

Crymmych Arms station from the overbridge looking south. *Oakwood Collection*

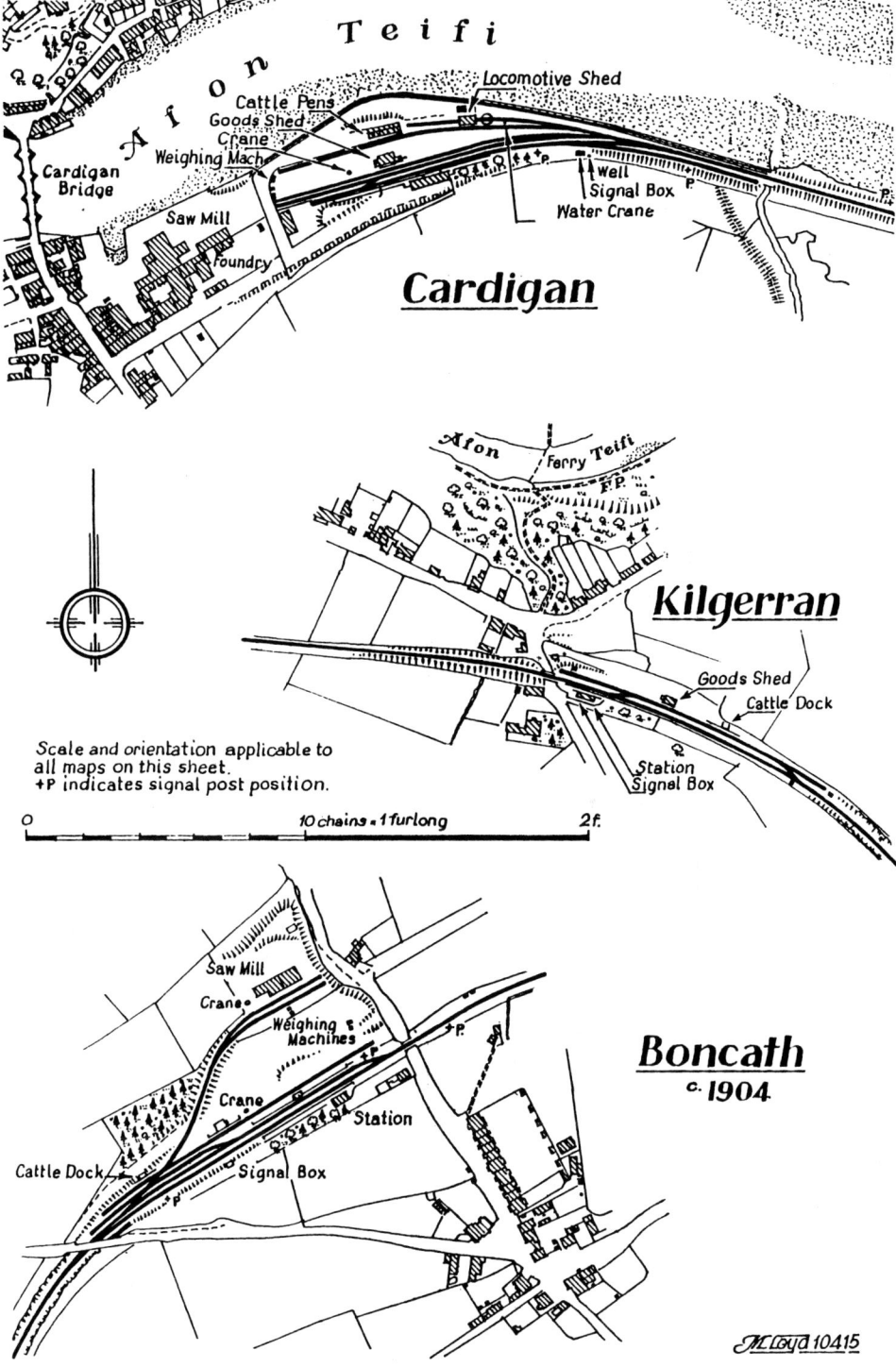

station (16 miles 34 chains from Whitland) was situated near the source of the Taf and in the shadow of the 1,297 ft high Freni Fawr, on the edge of the Prescelly mountains. The buildings were substantial, and right up to the 1960s a pillarbox was provided on the wall of the large station house on the up platform. Another facility on the up platform was a well which always gave ice cold water; a GWR cup was available for drinking purposes. After the tablet instruments were removed from Llanfyrnach, Crymmych Arms became the second tablet station on the line. Latterly it was the only intermediate station to be in the charge of a station master.

North of Crymmych the Cardigan Extension Railway climbed through a deep rock cutting to the summit before descending briefly on a gradient of 1 in 80 and rising again at 1 in 200 to a secondary summit about a mile and 30 chains beyond the station. By now the track was winding round a ledge on the hillside and giving magnificent views westwards to the Prescelly mountains, the reputed cradle of Stonehenge. On a clear day the view extended across the valley of the Afon Nyfer to the sea near Newport – overlooking the route the Crymmych–Newport extension would have followed had it ever been built.

The Cardigan Extension, meanwhile, negotiated a horseshoe bend and a remarkable series of sharp curves across the desolate countryside as it began its steady descent. Just over two miles from Crymmych the railway passed Rhyd-du, where once it was proposed to build a station. The earliest scheme for the Cardigan Extension provided for it, but on 29th February, 1884, James Walton, the then Engineer, told a questioner he had not included it on his plans because he had not been instructed to. Thus the station was never built, and the nearby village of Blaenffos was rather surprisingly left without any convenient stopping place. Just beyond Rhyd-du the Cardigan Extension Railway passed near Blaenffos and under the main Cardigan–Tenby road for the second time. A short distance further on a tributary of the River Teifi could be seen running through woods far below on the east side of the line, giving confirmation to the traveller that he was now across the watershed.

The next station, Boncath (20 miles 57 chains) was a crossing place and a tablet exchange station. The goods yard was quite sizeable, comprising three sidings on the down side, one forming a loop behind the down platform. Traffic consisted mostly of timber from the adjacent saw mills, rabbits and agricultural goods. Apparently the level crossing gates were demolished so often by accident that there was talk of doing away with them. In his two articles on the Cardigan line J.F. Burrell has pointed out that from the platform at Boncath it was possible to see the smoke of a freight train coming up from Cardigan for as long as a quarter of an hour before arrival. The many curves caused it to disappear and reappear at frequent intervals on the way. This was one of the most remarkable sights on a remarkable railway, because the line fell away from Boncath towards Cardigan on a gradient of 1 in 40 for nearly three miles. Climbing up this incline was hardly less exciting than the ever steepening climb up the Taf vale to Crymmych! Had the original route north of Boncath been built it would have kept to some higher ground and been more gently graded. It might also have been less attractive, because

An early view of Boncath station, view looking north to the crossing gates.
R.E. Bowen Collection

The station buildings at Boncath and Kilgerran were of similar design but with some differences in detail.
Lens of Sutton

A GWR 0–6–0PT No. 1613 pauses at Boncath station with a branch service.
Oakwood Collection

Boncath station and goods yard, looking south. *Oakwood Collection*

Kilgerran station, as seen from an up train, July 1958.

R.M. Casserley

Kilgerran station, view looking south.

Oakwood Collection

An up train from Cardigan crosses the overbridge approaching Kilgerran hauling 4-wheeled stock.   *T. David Collection*

Prairie tank No. 4556 standing at Cardigan at the head of a train for Whitland on 28th August, 1951.   *I.L. Wright*

Cardigan station, as seen from the approach road, this is now an industrial estate.
H.C. Casserley

No. 4550 backing on to 5.45 pm ex-Cardigan on 8th July, 1958. *H.C. Casserley*

2-6-2T No. 4541 shunts at Cardigan.
Oakwood Collection

0-6-0PT No. 1637 standing in front of Cardigan's modest engine shed on 8th July, 1958. Note the small turntable in front of the shed.   *H.C. Casserley*

A general view of Cardigan station and goods yard looking towards the buffer stops.
Oakwood Collection

6 Great College Street,
Westminster. S.W.
6th May, 1880.

To the Directors of the Whitland & Cardigan Railway.

Cardigan Extension.

Gentlemen,

Referring to your instructions of the 22nd January last to complete the Plans and Sections of the Cardigan Extension Railway throughout, I beg to inform you that the work is now sufficiently advanced to enable me to prepare Specification & Bills of Quantities in the event of your determining to advertise for Contracts.

It may be within the recollection of the Board that the plans supplied to me at the outset consisted only of tracings of the working plan and section from Crymmych to Boncath and of the last two miles into Cardigan; as to the intermediate portions I received no information whatever, beyond the use of the Parliamentary Plans. As this Section of the Railway comprises the bulk of the Earthwork and traverses the most difficult portion of the entire route I have been led to a careful study of the Authorised Line before determining upon its adoption between these points.

After my first inspection of the District and before the date of my appointment as Engineer I expressed great doubt as to the fact of the best line having been selected, and careful personal investigations have since fully confirmed my opinion. I have, in fact, been led to abandon the line altogether between Boncath and Bronhoil and to adopt another route which will effect a considerable saving in the amount of the work and length of line.

In determining the course of this Line I was led primarily to look at the question of crossing the dingle near Bronhoil as being the key to the position.

The Parliamentary Line approaches the dingle by a most circuitous route, which is apparent on the most superficial inspection of the plans, it is then carried over the same on an embankment with a maximum depth of 75 feet and a length of over 2700 feet. The forming an embankment of this magnitude would be a tedious and costly operation, and would most seriously interfere with the prospects of a speedy completion of the Railway. Under these circumstances, the questions I had to ascertain were: 1st. Whether the embankment was necessary, and 2nd. whether in the event of its being unavoidable it would be possible to reduce it.

As to the first point, if I had been called upon to lay out the line originally, I should not have selected the route adopted, but being restricted as to the general course of the Railway, I found it impossible to avoid crossing the dingle without unduly exceeding the Parliamentary powers.

As to the second point, by commencing at Boncath with a steeper gradient, I found it possible not only to effect a material reduction in the contents of the embankment, but to reduce the length of the line to be adopted to the extent of nearly half a mile; instead of following the Parliamentary gradient of 1 in 55 which necessitates carrying the line on a higher level, I have adopted an uniform gradient of 1 in 40, by this means I have been able to reduce the contents of the embankment to a minimum and by carefully selecting the intermediate ground have arranged for just as much excavation as will be required to form it, and no more. I estimate that a saving of over 100,000 yards of embankment has thus been effected, as the length has been reduced from 2700 feet to 1900 feet, and the height from 75 feet to 50 feet.

I have still further improved the line by increasing the radius of the curve at the dingle, from 12 chains to 14 chains, and by carrying it on the lower side of the farm premises, have avoided any interference with the approach roads; I have marked the course of this route on the Chairman's copy of the Parliamentary plan. I am aware that to the extent of altering the gradient from 1 in 55 to 1 in 40 I have not improved upon the old line, but with the shorter distance, the altered curves, and the great reduction in the amount of the earthworks, I claim to have effected a most material saving in expense.

I have been compelled to make a trifling deviation from the limits, but from all I can gather, the line now selected is likely to meet with the approval of the landowners and tenants.

As a set-off against reducing the gradient from 1 in 55 to 1 in 40 I propose altering the gradient on the working section of the Cardigan End from 1 in 41 to 1 in 50.

I have set out the line afresh between Crymmych and Blaenffos and have improved the curves and gradients as well as reduced the earthworks.

I enclose the altered section between Boncath and Cilgerrau.

Awaiting your further instructions.

I am Gentlemen,
Yours faithfully,
(Signed) JAMES B. WALTON
Engineer

J.B. Walton's report on the proposed Cardigan Extension, dated 6th May 1880.

the line as built ran for a mile and a half above a beautiful and heavily wooded valley towards Kilgerran, where the station was 24 miles and 32 chains from Whitland.

The station name of Kilgerran always gave some offence to the Welsh speaking people of the district. The correct name of the village was Cilgerran, and this appears to have been the station's original title. Probably only the perversity of Englishmen at Paddington caused the station to be given the anglicised spelling early in GW days. In any event, it was located not far from the River Teifi at the east end of the straggling village, which also boasted a castle. The facilities included a goods loop, goods shed and cattle dock, and latterly the station had the distinction of being the only one on the line to be unstaffed. Leaving Kilgerran the railway descended more gradually through pleasant wooded country and on embankments across the damp meadows of the Afon Piliau, a tributary of the Teifi. A run of three-quarters of a mile along the south bank of the river brought the railway into the County of Cardigan and the terminus, 27 miles 39 chains from Whitland, and 286 miles 32 chains from Paddington.

Cardigan station had one platform on which there was a large single storey station building. There was a run-round loop, and several sidings in the spacious goods yard. The small brick engine shed (erected in 1885), the water tank and turntable were situated near the water's edge, but ironically in spite of this location, there was an occasional shortage of water for the locomotives! To meet this need a special tank wagon was available for a a number of years to convey extra water to Cardigan. The yard was under the control of a small signal box, built of wood on a brick base, situated at the east end of the station platform. The whole setting by the Teifi formed a picturesque conclusion to a slow but delightful journey. The man who took the train to Cardigan was well aware that he had travelled!

The end of the line: a '16XX' pannier tank rests at Cardigan with a mixed train from Whitland. *Lens of Sutton*

Chapter Eleven
Locomotives and Rolling Stock

As mentioned in earlier chapters the Whitland and Cardigan Railway operated three locomotives, all constructed by Fox, Walker and Co. of Bristol. A very full account of these engines has already been published in the Railway Correspondence and Travel Society series *Locomotives of the GWR, Part 3 (Absorbed Engines 1854–1921)*. Accordingly it may suffice to set out particulars of these engines in tabular form. W&CR No. 1 *John Owen* (Works No. 170 of 1872) and W&CR No. 2 (Works No. 271 of 1875) were 0–6–0 saddle tanks of similar design. W&CR No. 3 (Works No. 340 of 1877) was a rather larger 0–6–0 saddle tank locomotive. All three were rebuilt by the GWR, and the dates at the top of each column refer either to building or re-building.

	No. 1 1872	No. 2 1875	No. 2 1887	No. 1 1894
Cylinders: in.	13 × 20 (oc)	dimensions	13 × 20 (oc)	14 × 20 (oc)
Wheels	3 ft 6 in.	similar to	3 ft 6 in.	3 ft 6 in.
Wheelbase	4 ft 10¼ in. + 4 ft 10¼ in.	No. 1, 1872	4 ft 10¼ in. + 4 ft 10¼ in.	4 ft 10¼ in. + 4 ft 10¼ in.
Boiler barrel	8 ft × 2 ft 10½ in. (outside)		8 ft × 3 ft 7½ in. (outside)	8 ft × 3 ft 7¾ in. (outside)
tubes	98 × 1¾ in.		200 × 1⅝ in.	190 × 1¾ in.
casing	3 ft 6½ in. × 3 ft		3 ft × 3 ft 9 in.	3 ft × 3 ft 9 in.
firebox	2 ft 11¼ in. × 2 ft 5½ in. × 4 ft 1 in. high		–	2 ft 4 in. × 3 ft 1 in. × 4 ft 6¾ in. high
Heating surface				
tubes	514.2 sq.ft		703.7 sq.ft	719.85 sq.ft
firebox	49.7 sq.ft		50.5 sq.ft	52.40 sq.ft
Total	563.9 sq.ft		754.2 sq.ft	772.25 sq.ft
Grate Area			7.13 sq.ft	7.2 sq.ft
Pressure			140 lb./sq.in.	150 lb./sq.in.
Tank			–	500 gallons
Weight (empty)			–	21 tons 8 cwt.
(full)			24 tons 13 cwt.	26 tons 1 cwt.

As originally built the saddle tank on locomotive No. 1 extended from the back of the smokebox. A dome was located over the firebox and an overall cab roof was provided. After the 1894 rebuilding at Swindon the saddle tank covered the boiler barrel only, the dome was placed much further forward and the cab and the bunker were rebuilt in GW style. The GWR number 1385 was carried on a plate on the cabside, whilst the name was on a small brass plate on the saddle tank. Prior to the rebuilding No. 1385 worked for a while as an 0–4–2ST. Afterwards it spent several years at St Blazey in Cornwall, before spending some time at Worcester. In August 1912 it was sold to the Bute Works Supply Co., subsequently going to Cornsay Colliery, near Durham. Long after the colliery had closed it continued to work there under the ownership of Ferens and Lovegrove Ltd. In about January 1952, it was sold to a Darlington firm for scrap.

Whitland & Cardigan Railway No. 3 as GWR No. 1387 seen here at Reading in 1925 before rebuilding.
Author's Collection

GWR No. 1331 seen here after rebuilding to lot 245, formerly Whitland & Cardigan No. 3.
Real Photographs

Locomotive No. 2 was rebuilt at Swindon in June 1887 – very soon after the GWR had taken the locomotive over from the Whitland and Cardigan. As further references to the engine emanate from Swindon rather than west Wales it is doubtful whether it ever returned to Cardigan. In later years the locomotive migrated to the West Country, and like No. 1 it did a spell at St Blazey. Eventually it was sold to the Bute Works Supply Co. in September 1911, and passed into the hands of the redoubtable Colonel Stephens for use on the East Kent Railway. It became EKR No. 1, and was later fitted with an enclosed cab. It was scrapped in 1934. Whilst on the Great Western this engine carried the number 1386.

Unlike the other two locomotives, No. 3 had inside cylinders and an enclosed cab and bunker. The saddle tank extended from the back of the smokebox to the cab, and initially the wheels were 4 ft in diameter and the wheelbase 5 ft 6 in. + 5 ft 6 in. Other particulars were as follows:

Year	1877	1902	
Cylinders	15¾ in. × 22 in. (IC)	16 in. × 24 in.	
Boiler barrel	8 ft 10 in. × 3 ft 4½ in. (outside)	8 ft 6 in. × 3 ft 8½ in. & 3 ft 9 in. (outside)	
tubes	129 × 1¾ in.	129 × 1⅝ in.	
casing	4 ft 8 in. long	4 ft 6 in. × 3 ft 5⅞ in.	
firebox	4 ft 2 in. long	3 ft 11³⁄₁₆ in. × 2 ft 11 in. × 4 ft 7 in. high	
		Tube heating surface	478.47 sq.ft
		Firebox heating surface	59.93 sq.ft
		Total heating surface	538.40 sq.ft

In 1902 the grate area was recorded as 11.84 sq.ft, the pressure as 100 lb. and the tank capacity as 700 gallons. The weight of the locomotive full was 31 tons 3 cwt. In June 1902, the engine was transferred from service stock to the Signal Department at Reading, where it remained until 1925. Throughout this period it carried its GWR service number 1387.

In February 1926 the locomotive was taken into the workshop for rebuilding under Lot 245. Although it had been added to service stock as No. 1331 by April 1926, it did not return to active service until 1927. The dimensions as a result of this rebuilding were:

Cylinders	[16 in. × 22 in. in 1896]	16 in. × 24 in.
Wheels		4 ft 1½ in.
Boiler barrel		8 ft 6 in. × 3 ft 5⅞ in. and 3 ft 5 in. (outside)
tubes		129 × 1⅝ in.
casing		4 ft 6 in. × 3 ft 6 in.
firebox		3 ft 11 in. × 2 ft 11⅞ in. × 4 ft 2 in. and 3 ft 3⅜ in. high
Tube heating surface		479 sq.ft
Firebox heating surface		56 sq.ft
Total heating surface		535 sq.ft
Grate area		12 sq.ft
Pressure		130 lb.
Weight (empty)		25 tons 18 cwt.
(full)		31 tons 12 cwt.

0-6-0 No. 1385, *John Owen*, formerly Whitland & Cardigan No. 1, before and after rebuilding by the GWR in 1894. The lower picture was taken at Worcester in about 1910.

Oakwood Collection

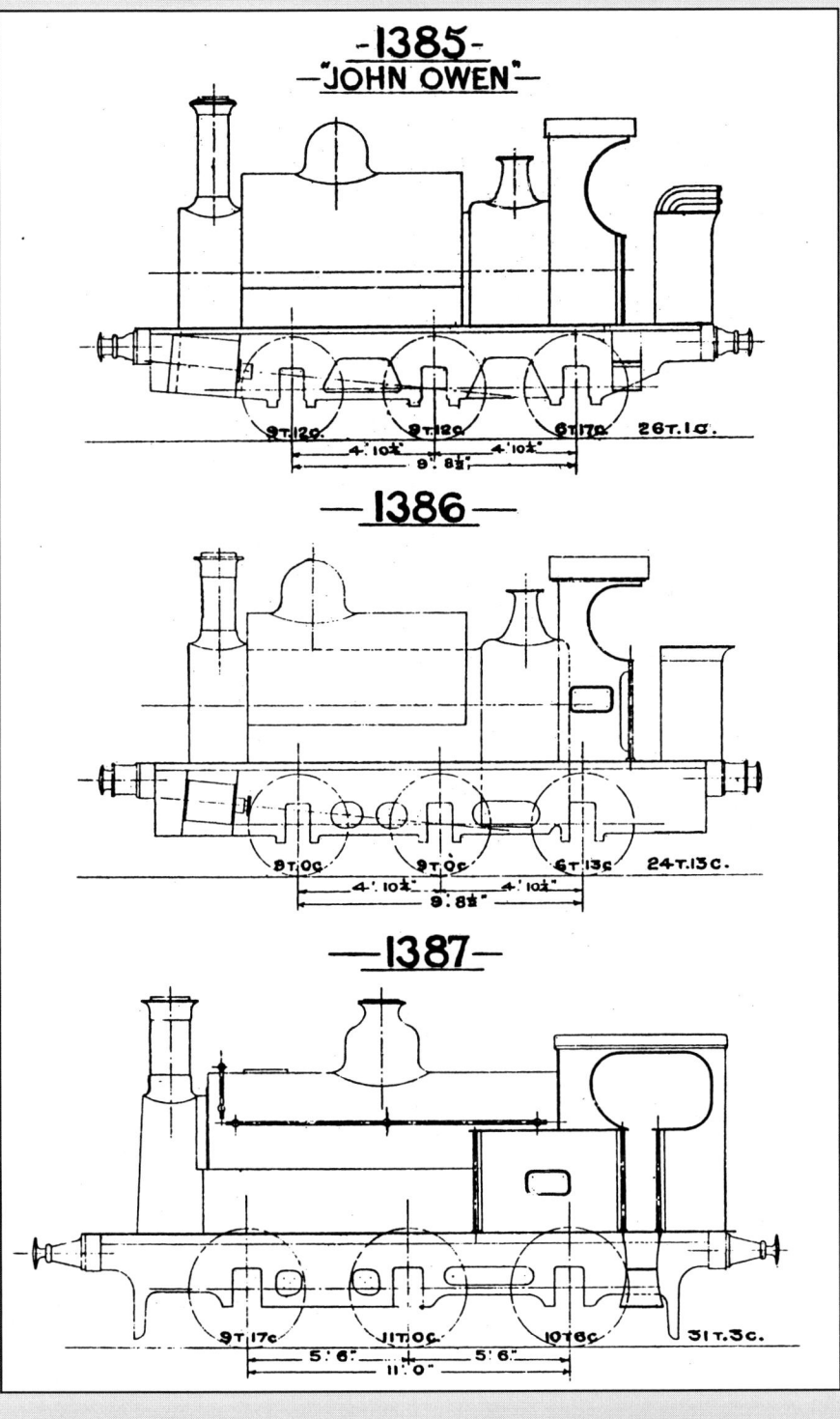

Whitland & Cardigan Railway No. 1 at Cornsay Colliery, Co. Durham still carrying *John Owen* nameplates.
F. Jones

Whitland & Cardigan Railway No. 2 as East Kent Railway No. 1 seen at Shepherdswell, Kent.
Dr J.R. Hollick

LOCOMOTIVES AND ROLLING STOCK

In the course of this rebuilding the closed-in cab was shortened, and the frames were lengthened at the rear to provide for a larger outside bunker. The general appearance of the engine was not changed significantly, although it now had a larger smokebox and a more angular dome cover. Early in 1946 the locomotive underwent its last major overhaul at Wolverhampton works; as a result it acquired 4 ft wheels once more, whilst the cylinders were now 16½ in. × 24 in. and the weight 31 tons.

Prior to its long stint with the Signal Department at Reading No. 1387 (as it then was) worked at Pontypool and Gloucester. As No. 1331 it worked at Weymouth for a few years, before being sent to Swindon and Oswestry. During its spell at Oswestry it was employed primarily on the mineral branches of the Tanat Valley. When it was withdrawn in January 1950, it was the last survivor of an interesting collection of old engines on the Cambrian lines around Oswestry. It was broken up in March 1950.

Extensive enquiries regarding the original livery of the locomotives and rolling stock of the Whitland and Cardigan Railway have not produced much result. All that seems reasonably likely is that the engines were painted green. The company records have more to say about maintenance, probably because this was a costly item. The locomotive shed at Llanfalteg was the home of all three engines before the opening of the Cardigan Extension, but it was not equipped to undertake heavy repairs. At some time in 1879, partly with a view to reducing expenses, arrangements were made for the GWR to give the engines necessary overhauls. By February 1881, it was reported that two locomotives had already been overhauled by the Great Western and that the third was now in the workshops. Even so it seems that locomotives were not automatically sent to Swindon for major repairs. In July 1882, No. 2 was being seen to at Llanfalteg by a boilersmith loaned by the GWR, the copper firebox having worn too thin for safe working. In February 1883, however, No. 3 needed repairs, but as neither the GW nor the makers could loan a boilersmith to do the job at Llanfalteg it was decided to send the engine to Swindon 'if the GWR will undertake to do the work.'

In the early days it appears that boilers and fireboxes were the most troublesome items on the engine. On 6th July, 1883, the Secretary told the Whitland and Cardigan Board that while No. 2 was having its firebox repaired he had borrowed a locomotive from the Maenclochog Railway 'for a few days.' Unfortunately no further details of this arrangement were given, but in a time of motive power shortage it is possible that the loan was for longer than the Secretary suggested. Certainly the Maenclochog could spare an engine because it had closed down on 31st December, 1882, and needed money from every available source.

Very occasionally the W&CR loaned its engines to others: for example in October 1884 a W&C engine was hired to the contractors Appleby and Lawton. In February 1885 No. 3 was sent away for repairs again, this time to Neath. In May 1885 two of the engines were said to have been repaired at Thos Peckett's Atlas Engine Works at Bristol, but by this date the company turned to the GWR for alternative motive power. Soon after the Great Western began operating the railway in September, 1886, a valuation of W&CR stock was made. No. 1 was valued at £450, No. 2 at £600 and No. 3 at £850.

Official Gloucester Wagon Co. photographs of the Whitland & Taf Vale coaches in pristine condition at completion of their construction. Photographed June and September 1875. *Courtesy H.M.R.S.*

Small Great Western tank locomotive types soon put in an appearance and the Whitland and Cardigan engines were moved away. Amongst the designs in evidence at the turn of the century were '19XX' 0–6–0 saddle tanks and Armstrong 0–4–2 tanks of '517' class. Pannier tanks were frequently seen as well, but during World War I one of the 0–6–0 saddle tanks, either No. 1939 or No. 1999, was stationed at Cardigan. On the freight side a 'Dean Goods' 0–6–0 regularly arrived at Crymmych with the monthly cattle train. This was probably the only working to bring a tender engine onto the branch with any frequency, but tender engines were never common. About 1950 a 'Dean Goods' was seen standing on the Cardigan line at Cardigan Junction, in the company of a composite coach and a Siphon 'G' van: this is the last known instance of the class on the W&C route. Larger tender locomotives were prohibited by virtue of the line having a yellow colour weight restriction.

For many years '2021' class pannier tanks were active on the line, and between the wars the more powerful '45XX' 2–6–2 tank locomotives appeared. These held sway on the Cardigan branch until the complete closure in 1963, although latterly they were supported by more modern pannier tanks in the '16XX' series. Amongst the engines seen on the railway in the post-war period were 0–6–0PTs Nos. 2011, 1637, 1648, 1666 and 2–6–2Ts Nos. 4550, 4557, 4569, 5550, 5571. In the final weeks of operation Nos. 4557 and 4569 were the most common performers on the railway.

Carriages

The Whitland and Taf Vale Railway owned six four-wheeled carriages, all constructed by the Gloucester Wagon Co. The first four were completed in June 1875, and comprised two composite coaches each having a first and two second class compartments, and a luggage compartment. The other two were brake thirds – that is to say comprising three third class compartments and a compartment for the guard. Pictures provide the only available clues on the details of the original livery. According to the recollection of a local man in old age the colour was a dark chocolate brown, the lettering being in gold. This is unconfirmed.

Two more coaches were supplied by the Gloucester Wagon Co. in September 1875, and these vehicles comprised three third class compartments and a luggage compartment. The order for these vehicles seems to be indicative as much of the desire of poorer people to travel as of the quantity of their accoutrements! When the 1886 valuation and inventory was made all the coaches were said to be 21ft 2in. long. Coaches No. 1 and 2 were valued at £45 each, No. 3 and 4 at £38 each and No. 5 and 6 at £33 each. After the opening of the railway to passengers in 1875 the *Carmarthen Journal* described the carriages as 'neat and commodious.'

Following the Great Western take-over of the Cardigan line standard GWR coach types began to appear. However it seems that there were also some curiosities. One elderly man from the area recalled hearing that coaches from the West London Railway worked on the line. In view of the fact that the West London owned no rolling stock this does not seem probable, but it is much more likely that the story refers to rolling stock from either the North London or the Metropolitan Railways some of which did find its way

Whitland & Taf Vale brake third coach No. 4.   Gloucester Wagon Co.

Cardigan Mercantile Co. Wagon No. 18 as new, before delivery. Gloucester Wagon Co.

into Great Western ownership. It has been said that the small and decayed portion of a van body placed by the cattle dock at Crymmych for many years had its origins on the Metropolitan Railway: it is more likely to have been from the GWR. A 4-wheel coach body resting in a field near Glogue until the 1960s was also probably from the GWR. On the other hand it is widely asserted that one of the original Cardigan line coaches was turned into a hound van for conveying the local pack of otter hounds. The body of this vehicle remained near the goods shed at Whitland for many years in use as a store.

The fate of the rest of the W&TVR carriages is unknown. In about the 1920s some Taff Vale coaches saw service on the railway, but by then GW coaches certainly were predominant. Bogie coaches were common by this time too. At closure the passenger rolling stock usually consisted of a two-coach 'B' set or one or two odd coaches, sometimes augmented by a General Utility Van of the Western pattern.

Wagons

These were all constructed by the Bristol Wagon Co., but no manufacturers' photographs are known to exist, and they have not been positively identified in any other pictures. In the circumstances very little can be said with certainty about this stock.

In October 1872, in anticipation of the opening of the line, the W&TVR ordered a 4-wheel goods brakevan and six 4-wheel open goods wagons. The brakevan was given the number 1, and the wagons were numbered from 2 to 7. Wagon No. 2 appears to have been the largest and heaviest of the batch, and No. 7 the lightest. The other four seem to have been of similar design.

In May 1874, as traffic developed, it was decided to order four more 4-wheel open wagons, but there is a minor puzzle about their numbering. The 1886 inventory reveals that Nos. 8 to 10 and No. 12 were open wagons, whilst No. 11 was a 4-wheel covered van – the goods van ordered by the company in October 1874, for use on the Crymmych freight service. As the other vehicles were numbered consecutively it seems that either the goods van was delivered before the last of the open wagons ordered five months earlier, or that one of the four standard open wagons Nos. 3–6 was written off in an early accident enabling its number to be taken over by one of the May 1974 batch. If so the open wagon bearing the No. 12 must have been a later acquisition. The livery of all these wagons remains a mystery, but following the precedent of the carriage stock paintwork it seems safe to assume that the wagons carried both the company's initials and the vehicle number.

A few other wagons are worthy of mention. Thanks to the records of the Gloucester Railway Carriage and Wagon Co. Ltd, details of four examples of private owner wagons may be given. In March 1903, William Thomas, Coal, Lime and Manure merchant of Whitland, obtained a five-plank 10 ton open wagon which was numbered 3. Painted the colour of lead, the letters were white shaded in black. In March 1904 the Cardigan Mercantile Co. Ltd, took delivery of a seven-plank 10 ton wagon, No. 18, which also referred to its owners as 'Timber, coal, culm lime and general merchants.' The livery was

Two Private Owner wagons associated with the Whitland & Cardigan line.
Gloucester Wagon Co.

black, the lettering being white. In the following month G.D. Owen, Coal and Lime Merchant of Cardigan obtained an almost identical wagon, also numbered 18, but painted dark red with white letters shaded black. Finally S.J. Phillips of Crymmych Arms, Coal and Lime Merchant, had a similar 10 ton wagon. This was supplied by the Gloucester company in September 1908, and given the number 7. It was painted black, the letters being white.

One other vehicle had a claim to be an item of Cardigan line rolling stock, although at a later date. This was the water tank wagon provided by the GWR in the 1920s or early 1930s to convey water to Cardigan where the supply was sometimes too low to fill the tank. Unfortunately no photographs of this wagon have so far come to light, but it has been described as a standard 4-wheel tank wagon, painted white with the initials GW painted in black on the side. The underframe was also black.

After the railway closed, farmer Dewi Owen, purchased Crymmych Arms, which he used as a base for his sub-contract from G.Cohen who were lifting the line. He converted this ancient Austin 10 for use as a railcar. An old maintenance trolley could be coupled to the bar at the back of the vehicle. This ad hoc arrangement, carried sleepers and rail to Crymmych for sale locally. *Courtesy A. James*

The band of the Cardigan Volunteer Corps and a 'good' crowd at Kilgerran station to celebrate the homecoming of Colonel Colby from the Boer War.   *Courtesy T. David*

A very busy scene with local Volunteers leaving Cardigan station by rail in World War I.
R.E. Bowen Collection

Chapter Twelve
Lead and Slate after 1870

Mention has already been made of the Llanfyrnach lead mine and the Glogue slate quarries, and in view of their importance they deserve further discussion. Whilst the association of Glogue with the Whitland and Cardigan Railway through the person of John Owen is obvious enough, the extent of the association of the Llanfyrnach mine with the railway is less clear. There are occasional references to the mine in the company's papers, especially in the early years, and there can be no doubt that the railway derived some regular traffic from it. This was probably the case right up to the closure of the mine in 1890, but the signs are that latterly rail traffic was reduced. In any event it seems possible that when the railway was opening to freight in 1873 there was a siding into the mine from a point about ¼ mile north of Llanfyrnach station. If so it cannot have lasted long because it is not shown on the first 6 in. Ordnance Survey map available, dated 1891. On the other hand this map does mark a tramway running through the mine workings which were spread out on both sides of the River Taf. By the time the next edition of the 6 in. Ordnance Survey map was published in 1907 the tramway was gone, and nothing more is known of it.

In 1871, whilst the Whitland and Taf Vale was under construction, Thomas Turner sold the mine to Messrs Lawson and Evans and they worked it for many years as a private business. Following a visit to Llanfyrnach in 1873 two correspondents reported to the *Mining Journal* on the state of the mine. Levels were then in operation at 38, 48, 58 and 68 fathoms, and they visited the first three, descending by ladders. The large size of the newer levels, the freshness of the air, the noise of pumping machinery and the wetness of some parts of the mine particularly impressed them, and they commented too on the polite, proud miners who worked by contract on eight hour shifts (beginning at 6 am, 2 pm and 10 pm) and earned about 25s. a week.

Lead miners frequently found that faulting in the rock displaced the productive lodes or veins, and when this happened they were confronted with the anxious task of locating the lode again. It appears that there may have been such an occurrence at Llanfyrnach in 1875, causing a crisis lasting many months. In any event the output slumped from 149½ tons of lead in 1873 and 80 tons in 1875 to 15 tons in 1876 and only 8 tons in 1877. Very fortunately a rich vein of ore had been discovered by 1878 and production soared. In that year 610 tons of lead were raised, and in 1879 the figure climbed to 1,064½ tons. This lode – the Water Lode – was to be the mainstay of the mine for the next decade, and production at the other lodes at Llanfyrnach was slight in comparison. The zenith of this exciting expansionist period was reached in 1881 when output amounted to 1,695 tons: subsequent annual figures were not nearly so high although in 1885 the mine managed to produce 1,439 tons, of which 188 tons were low-lead, high silver concentrates.

Unfortunately for the lead industry the period from 1876 to 1885 was marked by a disastrous slump in prices. Between 1850 and 1875 the price of lead averaged about £21 per ton, but in 1876 it fell to £16 per ton and for a while it continued to decline. The primary reason for the fall was competition from imported foreign ore, and even after the situation had stabilised somewhat the price was depressed, being only £13 per ton in 1888. In the circumstances Llanfyrnach might have suffered the fate of numerous other mines and closed down as a result of the slump. However by now it was one of the most important lead mines in Southern Wales, and it had the benefit of the recent discovery of a great deal of valuable ore. In the late 1880s, though, the position was less happy. After a gap in the records of about 20 years it appears that the mine was producing some zinc blende, the price of which was rising. In 1886 256 tons of zinc realised £438, whilst in 1888 155 tons of zinc realised £459. In contrast the output of lead was falling. In 1886 the production was 1,113 tons, in 1888 555 tons and in 1889 120 tons. In the last year, 1890, the output was a mere 10 tons.

At the time of the closure the price of lead had started to decline again, but the real problem at Llanfyrnach was that by 1890 the productive lode had been lost through faulting for several months. G.W. Hall records that as a very old man Mr Mansel Davies of Llanfyrnach passed on to him the story of the closure as given by his father, who had been in charge of the mine's workshops. Evidently the loss of the main lode reduced output to such an extent that the operating costs could not be covered. Eventually the owner, L.H. Evans, came down from London and tried to get the landlord to levy his royalty (believed to be 10 per cent) on profits and not on gross sales.

The negotiations were not successful, and to the dismay of local people the landlord allowed closure to take place rather than purchase the mine in anticipation of an improvement in trade. Although dampness and faulting made the mining difficult, one and perhaps two lodes at Llanfyrnach still contained valuable ore. In spite of this potential, in May 1891, the equipment was offered for sale, and subsequently most of the mine was dismantled. Today the remains of the boiler and Cornish engine houses are still to be seen, together with a few old buildings and a small chimney. Almost all the shafts are filled in, and the whole area is marked by dark tips, more or less overgrown.

Although the evidence of industry survives, it is hard to imagine Llanfyrnach in its heyday. Indeed, during the years of the Whitland and Cardigan Railway's independent existence the entire area around Llanfyrnach and Glogue must have been alive with activity. The slate quarries of Glogue were flourishing too. In the 1860s the proprietors of Glogue quarry traded under the title 'John Owen and Son', and were producing slate and stone for roofs and floors, hearth stones, window sills, pig troughs, cisterns and even coffins. At the time every new house in the district was made with materials from Glogue, but the business did look further afield as well. The products of the quarry were dispatched to many parts of the United Kingdom, and Miss A.L. Owen, a descendant still living at Glogue, recalls hearing that in the time of the younger John Owen the firm exported billiard tables to France and elsewhere. Although some of the slate was fragile, most of it was of excellent quality. The waste material was good enough for making bricks, and it also provided ballast for the railway.

Following the death of John Owen in 1886 the Glogue quarry stayed in the family, eventually passing by purchase to a nephew in 1890. The new owner died in 1901, but his son retained the Glogue estate until 1908 when it was sold to two local men, Griffith Thomas and John Rees of the shop at the nearby village of Tegryn. When Rees died in 1919 Glogue Farm was re-sold to the Owen family, but the quarry was acquired by a company believed to have been called The Glogue Slate Quarries Ltd. The new name does not appear to have meant much change in responsibility, at any rate at first: in 1920 Griffith Thomas was Manager and also a Director of the company. Latterly Mr J. Humphreys was Manager, and the Directors included Sir Hugh Thomas and a Mr Truscott, a London businessman.

Possibly the introduction of some outside management was significant in determining the fate of the quarry, because it is widely believed that the new men made a mistake in concentrating on production of roofing slates rather than in continuing to turn out the diverse range of products required locally. In any event the company has to be given credit for trying to increase production by investing in new equipment and by taking on more men. Whereas the number of employees in the years prior to World War I varied between 25 and 50 (some of whom came to the district from the slate quarrying areas of North Wales), by 1923/24 the number had increased to about 80. Meanwhile, a new machine shed was constructed in 1923, and soon after the company installed a new quarry engine. When the large new engine shed was opened early in 1925 the event was marked by a concert attended by almost all those associated with the quarry. As it transpired there was little to celebrate, because in March 1926 the quarry closed down. It was rather ironic that when this business failed it gave Mr Mansel Davies of Llanfyrnach an opportunity to build up a large road haulage business which came into competition with the railway. The firm out-lived the line and flourishes still, and in the mid-1970s its lorries were engaged in transporting hundreds of tons of waste from the quarry tips for road-making and other purposes.

After the closure of Glogue it seems that some of the equipment remained on site for many years, and to judge from a 1948 edition of the 6 in. Ordnance Survey map at that time the saw mill and the new buildings of the 1920s were still standing and most of the tramway in the quarry was intact. In view of the scrap drive in World War II this seems surprising, but even if correct, this equipment did not survive for long after it. It has to be said that in spite of their high reputation for accuracy, locally some doubt has been cast on the correctness of a few details depicted on the 6 in. Ordnance Survey maps. The First Edition, surveyed in 1888, and its revision, dated 1905, show something of the growth of Glogue quarries in the period: in the latter the two main quarries, both about 300 ft deep, are shown slightly enlarged, whilst the tramway system has received several extensions. Access to both quarries was by tunnels cut through the rock, but by 1905 a second tunnel had been cut to the westerly quarry, apparently to allow for the removal of material from the quarry at a deeper level. This feature has been doubted, but it appears on the 1948 edition of the map as well.

One error seems more certain: none of the maps show a rope-worked incline descending from a level on the top between the two quarries to the middle level, the level where the saw mill, machine shops and engine shed were situated. Nevertheless the incline existed, and it is shown in at least two surviving photographs of groups of quarry workers. Furthermore the upper part of it was still traceable amid slate waste in 1975. Its purpose was to link installations at the upper level, from which the quarry was partly worked, with those on the level below. A further incline descended to the bottom level adjacent to the Whitland and Cardigan line, about 16 chains long, running from Glogue station. At this spot there is believed to have been a loading platform for transhipment of slate from the trams used throughout the quarry into the standard gauge wagons. The W&C line to the quarry evidently terminated in two sidings, or a siding and a loop. At the time of the 1905 Ordnance Survey revision the junction of the quarry line with the Cardigan line just north of Glogue station was guarded by a signal box located on the opposite side of the line.

Within the quarry the tramway system was most extensive at the middle level, comprising a main line perhaps 600 yds long and other lines running from inside each of the main quarries out through the tunnels to the spoil tips. Although there has been some speculation as to whether a locomotive was ever employed in the quarry no evidence exists to support the idea. Horses may have been used to move the trams in earlier years, but those who recall the quarry when working say that the trams were invariably propelled by hand (except, of course, on the inclines). There is no contemporary information about the gauge of the tramway but on a visit to Glogue in August 1975, the writer located a very short portion of tramway track *in situ* and found it to be laid to the curious gauge of 2 ft 4 in. Several lengths of tramway rail were lying in the quarries, and those examined measured 1.7 inches across the base and had a height of 2 inches.

Before leaving the subject of lead and slate reference must be made to industry a little further down the valley of the Taf. In 1872 the *Mining Journal* carried an advertisement offering the 'mines of Rose Hill' for sale, and also 'valuable plant.' Rose Hill is close to Llanglydwen on the road climbing towards Llanboidy, but the mine shaft is now filled in. Locally this is reputed to have connected with an adit driven into the hill from a point near the railway, but whilst the entrance to the adit has collapsed the spoil dump is large enough to suggest that this might be true. Trial levels for lead were also cut at one or two other places near the railway at Llanglydwen, but were not developed.

In the 1870s plans were afoot for the opening of new slate quarries at Pencelli, between Llanglydwen and Rhydowen, and at Penlan, half a mile east of Rhydowen. Both appear to have been promoted by a Mr W. Bishop, who also had an interest in the nearby Elwin Valley slate quarries. Following a request from Mr Bishop in December 1878, the Board of the W&CR sanctioned the building of a tramway under its line for the convenience of the Pencelli quarry, Mr Bishop paying the entire cost of the works, maintenance and other expenses. Soon after a standard gauge siding was laid in to enable slate to be transferred to railway wagons for dispatch. In May 1885, the Directors of the W&CR were told that Bishop's siding at Pencelli had not been used for over twelve months, and they ordered it to be lifted. This directive possibly caused Bishop to provide the railway with sufficient traffic to justify the siding's retention, because the 6 in. Ordnance Survey map of 1891, surveyed in 1887, shows both the siding and loop on the west side of the Whitland and Cardigan line, together with the tramway incline descending from the quarry, and passing under the railway to reach it. By the time of the next edition of the map (dated 1907) the quarries were disused and the siding had gone, leaving only the spoil tips and a few buildings.

The Penlan quarry may have lasted an even shorter time. In January 1870, Bishop asked the W&CR Board about the possibility of building a tramway between this quarry and a transhipment point close to Rhydowen station. According to the Ordnance Survey map of 1891 the tramway was built, and comprised an incline at the quarry, and a line running approximately due west along the north bank of a stream to the tiny hamlet of Aberelwyn and a point on the railway just north of Rhydowen crossing. It is not clear if the railway provided a special siding for the traffic, and although the 1905 revision shows an extra siding at the station, by then the course of the tramway is marked as a footpath from Aberelwyn to the foot of the quarry incline and beyond. The quarry itself was clearly closed.

A 2-6-2T No. 5549 prepares to leave Cardigan with the 5.45 pm for Whitland, 21st August, 1961. *E. Wilmhurst*

WHITLAND & CARDIGAN.
(Single Line worked by Electric Train Staff.) WEEK DAYS ONLY.

Sections: Cardigan Junction and Llanglydwen / Llanglydwen and Crymmych Arms / Crymmych Arms and Boncath / Boncath and Cardigan

Crossing Stations: Cardigan Junction, Llanglydwen / Crymmych Arms, Boncath and Cardigan

DOWN TRAINS

Mile Post Mileage	Distance from Whitland	DOWN TRAINS	Station No.	Mixed Passenger arr. A.M.	Mixed Passenger dep. A.M.	Goods arr. A.M.	Goods dep. A.M.	Mixed Passenger arr. A.M.	Mixed Passenger dep. A.M.	Goods arr. P.M.	Goods dep. P.M.	Mixed Passenger arr. P.M.	Mixed Passenger dep. P.M.	Passenger arr. P.M.	Passenger dep. P.M.	Passenger arr. P.M.	Passenger dep. P.M.
258 74	M. C.	Whitland	3609	—	B 5 55	—	—	—	10 45	—	12 30	—	2 30	—	3 15	—	B 5 35
261 14	2 20	Cardigan Jct.	3613	6	6	7 27	7	10 50	10 55	12 35	12 50 CR 12 55	2 35	2 40	3 20	3 25	5 40	5 45
262 41	3 61	Llanfalteg	3778	—	6 15	7 42	7 47	11 4	11 15	1 0	1 30	2 45	2 49	—	3 34	—	5 54
265 1	6 7	Login	3780	—	6 25	7 57	X 8 15	11 13	X11 15	1 35	1 45	2 55	2 59	—	—	X 6 4	6 4
267 49	8 61	Llanglydwen	3781	—	6 31	8 20	8 25	—	11 21	CR	X 1 30	—	3 5	—	—	—	6 10
269 13	10 19	Rhydowen	3782	—	6 40	8 35	8 40	—	11 30	CR	Z 2 30	3 19	3 9	—	3 44	—	6 19
271 53	13 41	Llanfyrnach	3783	—	6 47	8 50	8 60	11 35	11 37	2 9	2 35	—	3 14	—	—	6 24	6 26
273 4	14 10	Glogue	3784	—	7 2	9 15	9 30	—	11 45	—	—	—	3 21	—	—	6 33	X 6 35
275 67	16 33	Crymmych Arms	3785	7 17	X 7 20	9 46	X10 40	11 57	P	2 45	X 3 30	3 41	P 3 43	—	—	6 47	6 48
276 52	17 58	Stop Board	—	—	—	—	10 42	—	—	RR	to	—	—	—	—	—	—
279 64	20 70	Boncath	3786	7 29	7 30	10 55	11 10	—	P 12 9	—	Cardigan	—	P	—	—	—	6 68
279 71	20 77	Stop Board	—	—	—	—	11 17	—	—	—	—	—	3 53	—	—	—	—
283 25	24 31	Kilgerran	3787	—	—	—	—	—	—	—	—	—	—	—	—	—	—
284 36	25 42	Stop Board	—	—	—	11 22	—	—	—	—	—	4 0	—	—	—	—	—
286 32	27 38	Cardigan	3788	7 37	—	—	—	12 16	—	—	—	—	—	—	—	7 5	—

Third Class only.

UP TRAINS

M. C.	Distance from Cardigan	UP TRAINS	Mixed Passenger arr. A.M.	Mixed Passenger dep. A.M.	Mixed Passenger arr. P.M.	Mixed Passenger dep. P.M.	Passenger arr. P.M.	Passenger dep. P.M.	Goods arr. P.M.	Goods dep. P.M.	Passenger arr. P.M.	Passenger dep. P.M.
		Cardigan	—	B 7 0	—	12 25	—	—	—	2 20	—	B 6 0
3 7		Kilgerran	7 19	X 7 21	—	12 34	—	—	2 45	X 3 50	6 19	6 21
6 48		Boncath	7 33	7 35	12 44	12 46	—	—	2 47 X	P4 16	—	—
10 79		Stop Board	P	—	—	—	—	—	—	P4 30	—	—
11 14		Crymmych Arms	7 42	7 44	—	12 50	—	3 44	3 25	X 3 35	6 33 X	6 35
13 28		Glogue	7 49	7 51	1 6	1 8	—	—	3 50	4 45	—	—
15 69		Llanfyrnach	7 58	8 0	—	1 14	—	—	4 15	4 55	6 42	6 44
17 19		Rhydowen	8 5	X 8 9	—	1 22	—	—	4 25	5 10	—	6 50
18 63		Llanglydwen	8 16	8 18	X 11 28	1 38	3 44	3 55	4 50	5 6	—	6 58
21 31		Login	—	—	—	—	—	—	5 15	6 35	—	7 4
23 71		Llanfalteg	8 26	8 31	11 34	11 36	—	4 14	—	6 45	—	7 14
25 42		Cardigan Jct.	—	—	11 42	11 44	—	4 18	5 20	6 50	—	7 23
27 38		Whitland	8 40	—	11 47	—	4 23	—	5 30	7 0	7 32	7 27

B To call at Llanglydwen, Login, and Llanfalteg for S.T. work only, unless other work can be done and enable Train to leave at booked time.
N Water and S.T. work only. Shunting at Glogue to be performed by 7.15 a.m. Whitland Goods.
Z Whitland Goods.

GWR Working timetable for September 1935 of the Whitland & Cardigan branch

Chapter Thirteen
Great Western Days

Once the Whitland and Cardigan had been absorbed into the Great Western, official records of the line became buried in the wider interests of the Paddington empire, and now they are much harder to trace. Although some information has come to light, and more may yet do so, it becomes difficult to set down the story chronologically. However, in another sense the task becomes easier in the years after 1890 because whilst there are few (if any) surviving pictures of the railway (other than rolling stock) in its short spell of independent operation, there are numerous fascinating photographs from the period of Great Western ownership. In any event with the winding-up of the W&CR the main part of the story is complete: for the next 70 years or so the railway simply peformed the job it was built to do, giving transport and communication to the little communities along its route.

In spite of the shortage of official information, by the turn of the century it is possible to incorporate another perspective in the account — that of memory. A number of elderly folk in the area still recall the 'Cardi-Bach' in the earlier days of Great Western operation, and in 1975 one, Mr J.J. Francis of Ferryside provided a fascinating impression of the line at that time. Referring to the scene at Whitland station he described the station master (who was also postmaster) as 'twenty-five stone, a huge man called Mr Williams.' There was a red letterbox at the station, and there was a postbox 'on the side of the guards van where people could post letters en route.' Recalling the first engine he saw coming into Whitland from Cardigan one afternoon he wrote 'I can remember her roar and her brass dome well polished.' Another vivid memory was of a saddle tank entering Crymmych Arms from Cardigan in about 1910.

The train Mr Francis remembered best comprised a GWR pannier tank painted green, with a neat three compartment coach (First and Third class, Ladies Only, No Smoking and so on marked plainly) and including a guard/brake compartment, then another three compartment brake coach and, usually, a parcels van. Other coaches might be added if the traffic required it, and generally the rolling stock was four-wheeled, although six-wheeled vehicles were seen from time to time. Sometimes, a GWR open 'gate' milk van was used to take parcels, but all mail would be loaded with the guard, valuable letters being locked away whilst heavy mail bags were chained to the guard's handbrake. For the young passenger the mail traffic was clearly a most fascinating feature of the line!

Another feature of the railway in independent days and very much later was the traffic for agricultural fairs and markets. In the 1890s local auctioneers described Crymmych's monthly market as being 'the best market in the Principality.' If that claim was extravagant there is no doubt that Crymmych became one of the important agricultural centres of West Wales, a fact to which the railway contributed and from which it gained a great deal of revenue. Before the end of the nineteenth century the cattle, horse and sheep fair was held regularly at Crymmych on the last Tuesday of each month, and as a general rule a cattle special was run from Carmarthen Junction to Crymmych. By the early years of the 20th century this was hauled by a 'Dean Goods' 0-6-0 — often No. 2321, 2323 or 2331.

Another fair was held at Henfeddau, a hamlet about three miles east of Llanfyrnach. The late William Lewis, one time station master at Llanfyrnach and at Llanglydwen and formerly a tracklayer on the Taf Vale line when it was being built, used to recall the cattle drovers being taken to and fro on the railway, and the sidings at Llanfyrnach and Crymmych being crammed with cattle wagons. Another, and more modest kind of livestock carried regularly was rabbits: in later years it was said that as many as two million rabbits per year were taken away by rail from stations on the North Pembrokeshire and Fishguard and the Cardigan lines. Even allowing for the rabbit's notable propensity to breed, this total seems extraordinary!

A line so rich in character as the Whitland and Cardigan could not avoid being commemorated in verse, usually in Welsh language. One incident taken up by a local rhymester concerned an accident on the railway between Login and Llanfalteg. By one account the accident involved a light engine alone, but the limited detail available suggests it might relate to the tragedy of the 6.30 pm down train on 25th August, 1885. At any rate both enginemen were killed. An attempt has been made to translate the rhyme, but the result was sadly unsatisfactory: the rhyme scheme of the original defied such treatment. Suffice it to say that the train ran on 'like a greyhound' through Dolau mawr, went out of control and crashed. Mr Llewelyn, a local railway gaffer 'flew like a crow' and 'Sophie the Tanner in her great grief was buried alive under coal dust.' If the detail seems confused the drama is obvious! The railways soon became a part of folk history, and the Rev. D.W. Thomas has recalled another instance of the line in local folk lore. In 1911 his grandfather entered the Eisteddfod at Llwynyrhwrdd near Glogue with an item linked to the W&CR entitled 'How to secure a late train.' He won the prize with this entertaining effort, and his grandson still has the ornate Welsh language certificate to prove it.

The 'Cardi-Bach' was a part of life, as local literature and legend testified. The men behind the railway were not forgotten either. On 18th December, 1912 there was a short ceremony by the Congregational chapel at Llwynyrhwrdd: it was to mark the unveiling of a monument to the memory of John Owen. The inscription was warm and sincere, even if it did strike a slightly materialistic note. It concluded with the words: 'The crowning glory of his life was the Whitland and Cardigan Railway, in the promotion of which he spent a large sum of money.' The fact that the monument was raised 26 years after his death may be seen as a measure of the affection and esteem he enjoyed around Glogue and in the Taf Valley.

Some of the staff on the line prior to World War I were notable characters. At Cardigan trains were in the care of Mr Challis, the driver, and John Thomas, the guard. At Whitland the regular crew was Joe Salmon, engine driver, and Mr Evans, guard. Joe Salmon of Llanfalteg was almost certainly one and the same as driver J. Salmon of W&CR days. However the issue is slightly confused because a driver named Tom Salmon is also reputed to have worked on the line at this time. At any rate the engine shed at Llanfalteg apparently did not close immediately after the GWR took over, even though the latter acquired its locomotive depot at Whitland. The shed had ceased to see regular use, however, before 1910.

The gangers and platelayers of the Cardigan line were a breed apart: in the words of the Rev. W.R. Nicholas 'unique, with their own special brand of culture.' In 1975 he recalled especially Cadifor Evans and T.R. Davies. The former was a well read man, renowned for his originality and humour. T.R. Davies, or 'Tomi'r Cwm' as he was called, was no mean poet, with many Eisteddfod prizes to his credit. He was also one of the coolest customers imaginable. The gangers had a small, low mechanical trolley to convey them and their tools along the line. One wet November morning in the early 1930s it went out of control on the stretch of line between Crymmych and Glogue, and it could not be stopped as it approached Glogue station. The gangers jumped off – that is all except T.R. Davies. He remained firmly seated on the load of sleepers which was on the trolley. Unfortunately the gates at Glogue were closed against it, but, in Rev. W.R. Nicholas' words 'the trolley continued on its way, smashing them to smithereens before coming to a halt just outside Station House. The lady who lived in that house, hearing the noise, came out to see what was happening. T.R. Davies was still safe, and fortunately sound, on the trolley, in the process of filling his pipe.' He turned to the wide-eyed lady and said quietly, 'it's a damp morning, isn't it?'

The sporting life along the line was good: shotguns were often carried in the engine cabs, and the families of the train crews lived well on pheasant, rabbit and fish. Services were sufficiently slow, it seems, to enable drivers to halt to collect a trophy! At least once in the inter-war period the authorities got wind of these activities and issued a directive to the effect that shotguns were not to be carried on the footplate. However no one on the railway appears to have been anxious about it. The men enjoyed a cheerful and amiable kind of life, even if they were not exactly prosperous. On one occasion driver Bowen had need of a dining table, and he found one at Cardigan. After a peaceful meal break around it on the station platform he and his companions loaded it carefully onto the engine's bunker for the journey home.

A different kind of incident took place at Crymmych Arms at about this time and mercifully was quite harmless. After doing a little shunting at the station the locomotive of the early morning freight left Crymmych for Cardigan without the train! The driver had travelled only a short distance before he realised his mistake, and fortunately the guard and the shunter at Crymmych managed to hold the wagons with the brakes pinned down.

Passenger traffic was never heavy, and the services changed little. In July 1938, the passenger timetable consisted of four trains a day each way, weekdays only, and stopping at all stations. Down trains left Whitland at 5.55, 10.45 am, 2.25 and 5.35 pm, the arrival times in Cardigan being 7.37 am, 12.15, 4.02 and 7.05 pm. In the up direction trains departed from Cardigan at 7, 10.15 am, 12.25 and 6 pm, reaching Whitland at 8.40, 11.44 am, 1.56 and 7.32 pm respectively. On Saturdays the 5.35 pm down and the 7.05 pm up trains ran five minutes later. The first down train of the day crossed the first up train at Boncath, whilst the 10.45 down crossed the 10.15 up at Llanglydwen. The last trains in each direction crossed at Crymmych Arms. A note was inserted in the timetable to the effect that Cardigan was the 'station for Gwbert-on-Sea (3¾ miles) and St Dogmaels

(1½ miles)'. The speed of these trains is worth noting: two of the down trains made the journey in 90 minutes, and the 10.15 up covered it in 89 minutes. Although the distance was only 27¾ miles these were probably the fastest scheduled services the line ever had!

The freight service at this period consisted of two trains a day in each direction on weekdays, and one each way on Saturdays. For a time too there was an additional weekdays-only freight service leaving Whitland at 6am and running to Boncath and back. In the war years some more trains were run, but on an 'as required' basis. The railway was generally busy: Crymmych had a large traffic in agricultural machinery, animal foodstuffs and coal, and every Monday a consignment of beer was received from Burton-on-Trent. At Cardigan too the sidings were often crowded in capacity, especially with coal wagons and vans of fertilisers. Even if the passenger trains were not full local people felt that the freight was enough to make the railway profitable. In the 1930s and 1940s this may have been true, but it is debatable. Certainly after World War II with the resurgence and growth in road transport the situation gradually deteriorated.

The winter weather on the Prescelly Mountains was often severe, and occasionally the railway was blocked by snow. Early in March 1947, however, the line between Crymmych and Boncath was blocked by deep snowdrifts for an entire week, and even when a snowplough reached the scene it could not break through. For several days the situation was critical. A freight train was trapped and in spite of the freezing conditions tank loads of milk went to waste, and a consignment of day old chicks was lost. Fortunately road access to Cardigan was just possible, but the townspeople were very conscious of their isolation. Eventually a hundred Polish troops were summoned from Aberporth (where they were stationed) in order to dig the railway clear. All in all the conditions on the line that winter were the most notable feature of the last year of Great Western ownership.

No. 4550 on arrival at Cardigan with the local service. *Oakwood Collection*

Chapter Fourteen
Nationalisation, Decline and Fall

On 1st January, 1948, the Cardigan branch of the GWR became part of the Western Region of the nationalised British Railways. In the period of British Railways ownership the passenger service consisted of four down and three up trains. The down trains left Whitland at 6.20, 11.35 am, 4 and 6.18 pm, reaching Cardigan at 8.14 am, 1.12, 5.36, and 8.02 pm. The up trains departed from Cardigan at 6.50, 10 am and 5.45 pm, and arrived in Whitland at 8.35, 11.40 am, and 7.29 pm. Occasionally slight variations were made in the timings, but the pattern remained the same. The time allowed for the journey varied from 96 minutes by the afternoon down train to 104 minutes by the evening trains in each direction. The trains called at all the intermediate stations, and latterly Llanfalteg, Login, Rhydowen, Glogue and Kilgerran were all known as 'halts'. Of these only Kilgerran became unstaffed; at the rest at least one person was required to deal with level crossing gates.

The goods service at this time was interesting. The first train of the day to Cardigan was the freight leaving Whitland at 5.40 am, and reaching the terminus at 8.43 am, having been overtaken at Boncath by the 6.20 am (or in earlier years the 6.30 am) passenger and mail train from Whitland. The first freight train in the opposite direction left Cardigan at 2.05 pm (1.20 pm on Saturdays) double-headed, the train engine being that from the down freight and the pilot engine being the one which had worked in on the 11.35 am (or, earlier the 11.30 am) passenger train from Whitland. At Boncath the pilot engine and an additional goods brake were detached, and put in charge of the 12.30 pm Whitland to Cardigan freight working. The goods train from Cardigan then proceeded southwards, followed at 3.50 pm by an extra goods service from Boncath hauled by the locomotive which had arrived there on the 12.30 pm train from Whitland. The last freight trip of the day left Cardigan for Whitland at 6.20 pm, thereby balancing the uneven passenger workings. About five years before closure, however, the services were rearranged to eliminate the 3.50 pm up train from Boncath. It should be added, though, that apart from the last trip in each direction it was common for passenger trains to run 'mixed' as and when required.

Latterly freight traffic was almost as varied as ever. Coal and fertilisers were conveyed to Llanfyrnach, Crymmych and Cardigan. At Kilgerran and Boncath the business was largely timber, and at Llanglydwen it was coal. A lot of milk went by rail, and although there was some decline in cattle traffic even in the late 1950s plenty of cattle wagons were to be seen at Crymmych. In spite of this volume of goods traffic, and some steady custom in passengers from villages devoid of any other public transport, it became obvious in the 1950s that the days of the railway were numbered. Even the additional traffic to Cardigan in the summer months was not sufficient to safeguard the future of the line which was, by any reckoning, expensive to operate. The branch was long and sinuous, and the gradients severe, causing additional wear on locomotives and rolling stock. The numerous level crossings on the route all required employees to look after them, and signalmen or goods yard staff were needed at Llanglydwen, Crymmych, Boncath and Cardigan. In the circumstances it was not surprising that by

1961 British Railways had decided the services were uneconomic. In February 1962, BR submitted proposals for withdrawal of the passenger service to the Transport Users' Consultative Committee, and subsequently these were approved, subject to the provision of satisfactory alternative bus services.

The passenger service was withdrawn at the end of the summer timetable, that is to say with effect from 10th September, 1962. As there was no Sunday service the last trains ran on Saturday, 8th September. After some weeks with more passengers than usual, on the final day the railway saw more travellers than almost anyone could remember. Amongst the passengers though was Herbert James, aged over 80, who could recall his 'marvellous trip' on the first journey to Cardigan on 1st September, 1886. He was the only person to travel on the first and final trains. When the last train pulled out of Whitland it carried about 50 passengers; by the time it reached Cardigan it had about 500 crammed on board! After many whistles, cheers and laments the train returned slowly to Whitland, passing sight-seers at all the stations on the line. The locomotive, appropriately enough, was one of the '45XX' type of 2–6–2 tank locomotives which had been a familiar sight on the railway for many years. The driver was Mr Gilbert Lye and the fireman Mr O. Glover.

On the following Monday Midway Motors began a new bus service linking intermediate points along the route of the railway. The buses left Cardigan at 7 and 10 am and 3.55 pm, and Whitland at 10 am, 1 and 6 pm. Some said that these times were not so convenient as those of the passenger trains. Certainly the buses proved to be every bit as slow as the railway, and they did not prosper. After two or three years the service was discontinued, and a century after John Owen first took the initiative most of the Taf vale was left without any public transport at all. Ironically the most direct route from Cardigan to Carmarthen was by bus via Newcastle Emlyn, roughly following the route of the original Carmarthen and Cardigan Railway!

By 1973 Midway Motors was providing a meagre service south from Cardigan. Buses departed from Finches Square as follows: 10 am Mondays–Saturdays for Hermon (near Glogue), with a connection at Crymmych for Tenby; 1 pm Wednesdays and Saturdays only to Hermon; 4 pm Mondays–Saturdays to Hermon, and 5.55 pm Mondays–Saturdays to Crymmych. On Tuesdays and Fridays only the 10 am and 4 pm journeys were extended to Glogue and Llanfyrnach. The buses returned from Hermon Post Office at 10.55 am, 1.40, 4.55 and 6.40 pm (Saturdays only). These timings were not invariably helpful. By way of example, the 4.55 pm bus from Hermon reached Cardigan at 5.30 missing the 5.25 pm bus to rail connections east from Carmarthen. The timetable made a day trip to Crymmych from anywhere other than Cardigan a virtual impossibility for those without private cars!

When the passenger service ceased British Railways reduced freight facilities considerably. The timetable provided for only one train each way on Mondays, leaving Whitland at 10.35 am and returning from Cardigan at 3 pm. On other weekdays there were two trains each way at 5.40 am and 1.20 pm from Whitland, and leaving Cardigan at 10 am and 5 pm, thereby enabling Cardigan shed to be closed. Llanfalteg, Login and Rhydowen 'halts' were also closed completely, and trains stopped at Glogue only to take water. 'Smalls' traffic was withdrawn from Llanglydwen, Llanfyrnach and Boncath, this traffic having finished at Kilgerran when it became unstaffed some years before. Most of the staff were retained at Crymmych and Cardigan for a while, although further cuts were known to be inevitable. They came soon enough, because the freight service ceased with effect from 27th May, 1963. One or two trains ran over the line after that date to collect materials and to clear wagons, but as late as August 1963, two Great Western type General Utility Vans were to be seen on the weedy tracks at Cardigan station. The few staff remaining were now given the option of moving to other jobs on BR or being made redundant. The last man employed on the line by British Railways was Mr E. Stephens, a checker, who was at Cardigan until as late as November 1964.

Track lifting operations began in December 1963, and were completed by July 1964, the contractors being G. Cohen Ltd. Some of the trackwork was removed by rail and used elsewhere on the Western Region of British Railways. Unfortunately no records survive of the equipment used on the melancholy task of demolition, but it is believed that a small diesel or petrol locomotive was used with the track lifting train. If so this was almost certainly the one and only time the railway saw a train which was not steam hauled – in itself quite a comment on the fate of the line!

At the end of 1964 the Whitland and Cardigan Railway was deserted and desolate, and BR began to consider the sale of the land. Later in the 1960s the land was disposed of, mostly to local farmers or other adjoining landowners. By 1975 the scene had changed considerably, and in many places it was hard to imagine the W&CR as a going concern. At Cardigan Junction a thin line of ballast and weed was all that was left to show where the branch had turned off to the north. At Llanfalteg one of the crossing gates and the station platform survived, but all the buildings had gone. Login station had fared better because the big station house, renamed Taf Alaw, was in private occupation. Although the trackbed was filled in to platform level, the booking office was largely intact and in use as a store. The gate on the north side of the level crossing was also intact, and the presence of two iron goods van bodies on the station site was another reminder of its railway associations. At Penclippen crossing the gates were still *in situ*, and in good condition.

Further north the station at Llanglydwen was also nearly complete. The signal box had gone, but the station house still showed evidence of a Great Western colour scheme. In contrast the scene at Rhydowen was one of dereliction. The station platform was very broken down and overgrown, and the only building on railway land was a platelayers' hut in use as a shed. The station house adjoining the line was painted in blue and white and here again crossing gates survived. At Llanfyrnach they did not. The station was in use as a private house, but the trackbed was filled in to provide a lawn. Railway van bodies remained on part of the platform, but to the north the goods yard was used for storage and scrap. Parked lorries bearing the title Mansel Davies Ltd, Llanfyrnach, were a reminder of the local firm which had become successful in the road haulage business well before the railway died. Indeed, it probably helped to kill it!

In 1975 there was not a great deal to see at Glogue. There were no buildings left on the deserted platform, although the station house by the level crossing was still inhabited. One gate remained at the crossing where T.R. Davies had his remarkable escape 40 years before. On the hillside above the village familiar screes of grey slate marked the site of the Glogue quarries, from which contractors were busy removing material. Nearby a few rotten sleepers indicated the course of the largely overgrown quarry line. The station at Crymmych Arms was more interesting. On the up side the station house had been renovated and was in private hands. Chickens were running between the platforms, and the down side buildings were then advertised as being in the possession of Cemaes R.D.C. The signal box had gone, and the goods yard was in use as a car park. Beyond, the cattle dock and pens remained, together with a remnant of an early railway coach. North of the brick-built overbridge the deep, steep-sided cutting was very wet, and partially filled in by tipping. In the 20th century Crymmych Arms itself has expanded considerably, but the area near the old station still has a number of wooden and corrugated iron buildings, some bearing elderly enamel signs. The old Crymmych Arms Inn now serves the motorist, but despite the expansion part of the place at least retains something of a frontier town atmosphere.

The two intermediate stations on the Cardigan Extension Railway have decayed. The station building at Boncath was partially boarded up in 1975, although traces of GWR paint remained and a notice proclaiming 'you can telephone from here' projected incongruously from the brickwork. The derelict goods shed and the overgrown platforms were still standing, but the only sign of signalling was provided by a concrete signal post buried in the boscage. Both crossing gates were *in situ*. At Kilgerran the station building had gone, but the platform, cattle dock and goods shed still stood. The yard was largely covered in timber and building materials belonging to D.G. Thomas & Sons Ltd, who occupy the site. At Cardigan the station site was also in commercial use, but here the station building was in good repair as the offices of J.E. Howard Ltd, a firm dealing in agricultural machinery and materials. Apart from the loss of the signal box and of fencing the station was intact. A sign saying 'Gentlemen' was still to be seen, and two other BR enamel notices had been painted over, 'Stores' and 'Manager's Office'.

Across a rather muddy yard the goods shed appeared to be unchanged, and some other concrete and corrugated iron sheds in the goods yard survived, being in use for agricultural merchandise and fishing equipment. The old locomotive shed was, however, demolished. The site of the turntable pit was filled in with rubble and broken slates, probably the last remains of the shed building. At the eastern extremity of the station site the trackbed was fenced off to prevent trespassers entering the Teifi Nature Reserve alongside the river. On a brighter note, though, the view across the calm waters of the Teifi was as picturesque as ever, the most prominent landmarks still being St Mary's church, the district hospital and, further west, the walls and mound of Cardigan Castle.

Between 1964 and 1975 the nearest railway to Cardigan was at Newcastle Emlyn, at the terminus of the branch which began life as the Carmarthen and Cardigan Railway. Rather curiously, the passenger trains to Newcastle Emlyn were withdrawn in September 1952, ten years before the passenger trains to Cardigan, but the goods service to Newcastle Emlyn lasted ten years longer than that between Whitland and Cardigan. The Carmarthen–Aberystwyth line, which used the C&CR route as far as Pencader, lost its passenger trains on 22nd February, 1965, and a few months later Llandyssul, the former C&C terminus, lost its freight facilities. Complete closure came with the end of freight traffic to Newcastle Emlyn on 28th September, 1973. Although the Teifi Valley Railway Preservation Society campaigned for retention of the line, by the end of 1975 most of the C&CR was lifted. Preservation plans were then confined to a section of the route near Bronwydd Arms, making the prospect of trains ever returning to the Teifi Valley seem remote indeed. In railway terms Cardigan is as isolated now as it was before the advent of John Owen and the Whitland and Taf Vale Railway. Clynderwen station is still open, but only as a halt. Such is the decline of railway business that the withdrawal of all passenger services west of Carmarthen, or even Swansea, is now a possibility. The Whitland and Cardigan Railway was a creature of its age, and by present standards it is amazing that it lived so long.

Cardigan Station on 3rd August, 1963, almost a year after closure. Two utility vans atand at the platform, but on the right are the first signs of track lifting.

Author

The sad state of Crymmych Arms station, view looking north, 1975. *Author*

Penclippen crossing seen in May 1984. *Author*

Boncath station building, in its delapidated state August 1987. *Author*

Chapter Fifteen

POSTSCRIPT, 2020

Forty four years have elapsed since this book was first published, and no less than fifty eight years since the "Cardi Bach" closed to passengers, so it is hardly surprising that fresh insights and information have emerged relating to this story. The process has been helped by a small group of local enthusiasts and railway modellers constituting the "Cardi Bach Railway Society", aiming both to commemorate the old railway, and to share their varied knowledge and expertise. In 2019 members were very largely responsible for the creation of a small museum at Login, much assisted by the goodwill of Peter Towns, owner of the former Login station, part of which is now a small café. A fine achievement for the small group, this museum may be opened on a few advertised occasions, and also customers at the café will usually be allowed to visit on request. The museum is housed in a robust shed adjoining the former station platform, and comprises a fine array of photographs, superb models of the old stations at Cardigan, Kilgerran and Boncath, and a number of interesting artefacts. Amongst the latter may be seen the Cardigan signalbox nameboard, and also a large blue enamel station running-in board, "Cilgerran". This item is thought to have been made in or about 1885, shortly before the opening of the Cardigan Extension from Crymmych Arms. If it was ever actually erected, its display was very probably short-lived because the GWR chose to anglicise the place name, and calling it "Kilgerran". The "Cardi Bach" ran through portions of Carmarthenshire and Pembrokeshire, as well as Cardiganshire, but as Login is located in Carmarthenshire the museum was formally opened by the chairman of that County Council on 14th May, 2019.

These additional notes relate to several different aspects of the "Cardi Bach" story:-

The Early Years

The first chairman of the Whitland & Taf Vale Railway, Stephen W. Lewis, was raised in the village of Llanboidy, seven miles north of Whitland and about three miles south-east of Llanglydwen. Like his friend John Owen of Glogue, he had gone to London in pursuit of commerce and prosperity, and he seems to have been very successful. As a native of Llanboidy, Stephen Lewis undoubtedly knew the remarkable local squire, small of stature and large in spirit, Walter R.H. Powell of Maesgwynne. Like many country gentlemen, Powell enjoyed horses and hunting, but he also had bold ideas and (in the context of the times) some radical opinions. The latter undoubtedly helped him later become the Liberal MP for West Carmarthenshire in 1880. In the 1870's, though, Llanboidy was a larger village than nearby Whitland, but as Whitland had become a railway junction, it was far more likely to grow. In that era proximity to a railway was akin to proximity to civilisation itself, and so Powell really wanted a railway for Llanboidy. Accordingly, when the W&TV Bill came before Parliament, Powell attempted to have the line re-aligned to run close to his village.

Unfortunately for Powell, there was one very obvious difficulty. The plan for the railway was to build up the valley of the Taf, whilst Llanboidy was in the hills two or three miles to the east. As the main purpose of the line was to serve the Glogue quarries, and there was no significant source of revenue at Llanboidy, there was no real reason for the company to divert the line up into the hills towards the village, before taking it back down the valley of the Tegin to reach Llanglydwen. The civil engineering required for such a diversion would have added significantly to the substantial costs involved, and in any event raising the necessary capital for the line was never going to be easy. As a result, W.R.H Powell was disappointed, although naturally several villages and hamlets in the Taf valley were pleased to see the railway create a new and time-saving line of communication. In 1877 Powell was sadly disappointed again, when an entirely separate scheme was put forward, for a railway running from Whitland to Pendine, on the Carmarthenshire coast. This project envisaged a branch running east from Whitland, but Powell hoped that another branch might be built from it, this time running north towards Llanboidy, following the Afon Glonw, a tributary of the Taf. When the intended standard gauge line failed to materialise, in 1882 a cheaper narrow gauge version was proposed. This also failed, and Powell's dream died with it.

According to *The Welshman* newspaper for 2nd August, 1872: "A temporary branch has been made to the waste from Glogue slate quarries where the contractor obtains ballast, and he is now ballasting the line between Llanglydwen bridge and Glogue." In June, 1873, the Whitland & Taf Vale minutes mention an incident in June, 1873, when loaded wagons ran away from the quarry and derailed at Llanfyrnach. It seems clear that the temporary siding diverged from the main running line several hundred yards south of Glogue and ran north directly up to the quarry slate tips, where the quarry waste was loaded into the contractor's wagons. The mishap probably caused the temporary siding to be abandoned as soon as practicable in favour of an alternative siding facing Crymmych, from points just north of Glogue station. Within a few years the end of the temporary siding alignment had been covered by quarry spoil, but remarkably, as late as 1981 it was still possible to trace part of the route of the old siding across overgrown ground to the south of the quarry.

No official track plans appear to have survived from the W&TVR period, apart from a plan of Taf Vale Junction at the time of the Board of Trade inspection in 1873. Col. Rich's second inspection of the route to Crymmych in 1878 revealed several faults, and in spite of the fact that the railway was in regular use, the Board of Trade continued to issue monthly notices to postpone the opening of the line! When the W&TVR was brought under the control of the Great Western it was soon re-laid to a higher standard with slightly heavier rail. A second platform and a passing loop was provided at both Crymmych Arms, and Llanglydwen, and as the two quarries near Rhydowen were soon abandoned there was no lasting need for sidings to

Login station in May 1984. *Author*

Llanglydwen station being used as a coal yard photographed in May 1984. *Author*

serve them. After the relaying the locomotive shed at Llanfalteg was less used, and the adjacent passing loop was disconnected at the north end. When built in 1873 the shed measured 60 ft. by 15 ft, and it had an inspection pit 46 ft. in length. The building had a slate roof, and wooden doors, and was extended in 1876 by the addition of an engineman's room. A year later a coal stage was installed (without crane); water was obtained from a pipe adjacent to the level crossing. The shed was redundant by 1897, but was rail connected until 1913, being for many years in the care of the Civil Engineer's Department. After 1897 the GWR had possession of the Pembroke & Tenby Railway's shed at Whitland, and thereafter used it to maintain the locomotives used on the Cardigan branch services. The original P&T structure was destroyed by fire in 1901, and was replaced by the shed building from Letterston in 1902. This was later rebuilt, but eventually it was dismantled not long after the final closure of Whitland shed in 1966.

The Penlan (Elwyn Valley) quarry has been mentioned as a short-lived and unsuccessful enterprise near Rhydowen, opened in or by 1879. The tramway serving the quarry was laid to a gauge of 2ft. 6ins and was just under a mile in length, ending at an incline up to the quarry workings. It is thought that the line was horse-worked below the incline, but no description of the line in operation has emerged. Even so, as late as 1891 the tramway was depicted on a printing of the 6" O.S. map.

More light was cast upon the history of the Glogue quarries in an article published in 1983, and written by Gordon and Mary Tucker (*National Library of Wales Journal*, Vol.XXIII, No.2, p.141). The authors noted the high cost of road transport prior to the building of the railway, and observed that once John Owen (junior) took charge the quarries experienced a period of considerable development. Whereas in 1861 31 men were employed, by 1871 there were 52 skilled workers. By 1881 the number had dropped back to 30, with some reduction in output. In 1885 production was said to be a modest 2,000 tons. Following John Owen's death in 1886 the quarries were run for a time by the Glogue Brick and Slate Works Ltd., although their plans to establish a brick works at Glogue never materialised. Between 1906 and 1912 some 15 to 18 men were employed producing slates under the direction of the Glogue Quarry Syndicate, but the formation of the Glogue Slate Quarries Ltd (1919 – 1926) lead to some serious investment and re-equipment.

The Cardigan Extension

In August, 1878, the *Western Mail* noted that Alfred Weekes Szlumper was the engineer present at the cutting of the first sod "on the railway to Cardigan". A.W.Szlumper (1858 -1914) was the younger half-brother of J.W.Szlumper (1834 -1926), and for a time his pupil and assistant. In spite of Alfred's youth, J.W.Szlumper evidently had enough confidence in his ability to make him Resident Engineer on the Cardigan Extension, although this may have contributed to the difference of opinion with the W & C.R. board in the autumn of 1878. Even so, A.W. Szlumper, like his elder brother, went on to greater things, eventually becoming Chief Engineer of the London &

South Western Railway, and later the Southern Railway. Alfred's son, Gilbert (1884 – 1939) was also employed by the Southern Railway, rising to the position of General Manager between 1937 and 1939.

Some work had been carried out on the Cardigan Extension by the time the Great Western board met on 29th May, 1879. They had received a report on the Whitland & Cardigan Railway and its parlous finances, and decided that they could not consider purchasing the company, but that they would be willing to discuss any suggestions the company made regarding a Working Agreement. From the Great Western's point of view, the fact that the line then terminated at Crymmych was a distinct problem. Some GWR officers had travelled over the line and considered "that as long as the line terminates where it does, the traffic is not likely to increase." They also felt that additional staff would be needed, and the local engineer declared that "the line in many parts is in bad order, and within five years it must be entirely relaid." Accordingly, the officers considered that "if we took over the line, working expenses would more than equal the entire receipts unless (which is unlikely) revenue materially increases."

Added to this concern, the Great Western board was invited to consider the possibility that through traffic to and from the W & C.R. might not justify their working the branch on terms which otherwise would not be remunerative. It was concluded that:-

> A railway to Cardigan must undoubtedly be constructed some day, but it is stated by the Officers that the Whitland route as proposed does not go through anything like so good a district as that projected in connection with the Carmarthen & Cardigan via Llandyssul – though it is probable as the Whitland & Cardigan line has actually been commenced and the landowners and others are stated to be very favourably disposed towards it that that will eventually be the route by which railway accommodation with Cardigan will eventually be effected.

For some time the engineers were delayed by the need to stabilise the railway trackbed crossing marshland by the River Teifi on the approach to Cardigan. After this was resolved, track-laying was completed in the summer of 1885. The achievement may well have been tinged with relief, because on 10th August the company took the liberty of operating a passenger excursion of very doubtful legality, briefly reported in the local press under the heading "Excursion to Tenby". The report continued "This excursion, the first over the Cardigan Extension railway, took place with much success on Monday last, about 350 passengers availing themselves of a cheap trip to the Queen of Welsh watering places". A week earlier the newspaper had carried an advert headed 'Opening of the railway to Cardigan for goods traffic', which also enabled the Boncath Mercantile Company to announce their 'new and specially designed covered lime trucks'. The advert concluded with a reference to the Mercantile Company as 'the first freighters over the Extension Railway to Cardigan direct.'

On 22nd June, 1886, the Whitland & Cardigan did turn to the Board of Trade to request an inspection prior to the formal opening of the extension, also asking that the restrictions imposed in 1869 relating to the speed of trains and weight of engines be lifted, so that the two portions of the line might be worked as one ordinary railway. Colonel F.H. Rich duly conducted an inspection on 5th July, and noted that the southern end of the line had been re-laid with Vignoles rails weighing 75lb/yard, and the underbridges strengthened. Work on a new station building for Llanglydwen had only just begun, and smaller buildings were still needed at Llanfalteg and Boncath. Lamps were still needed at several stations, and a lodge was required for the gatekeeper at Penclippen level crossing.

From the company's point of view, Col. Rich's report was depressing. The W&CR had expended its capital, and they had no option but to turn to the Great Western for assistance. Fortunately the GWR advanced the necessary funds to enable the work to be put in hand, and gave the Board of Trade an undertaking that the works specified by Col. Rich would be completed within six months. In response to the request to allow increased train speeds, Col. Rich declared that they should be limited to 20 mph. The Chief Engineer of the GWR took this to mean an average speed, including stops, of 20 mph, and advised his board accordingly, with the proviso that any undertaking given on the matter should only relate to those portions of the line subject to severe curves and gradients. On 13th August, 1886, however, the W&CR and the GWR gave a joint undertaking that the speed of trains between Whitland and Crymmych Arms, and on the extension through Boncath and Kilgerran, would not exceed an average speed of 20mph. They also agreed that the whole line would be worked by train staff and ticket, in conjunction with the block telegraph. On 26th August the W&CR engineer, J.B.Walton certified that the necessary works had been carried out, with the exception of certain level crossing gatekeeper's lodges. After the appropriate undertakings had been given, the Board of Trade authorised the opening of the railway on 31st August. (National Archives, MT6/448/7)

The formal opening of the Cardigan Extension was overshadowed in some Welsh newspapers by proposals to open a much greater wonder – the long awaited Severn Tunnel – to goods traffic. On 1st September, 1886, though, *The South Wales Daily News*, devoted considerable space to activities in Cardigan on the previous day:-

> On Tuesday was celebrated the opening of the extension line from Crymmych to Cardigan, and from today the GWR Company will take over the entire line from Whitland to Cardigan, and henceforth work it for passenger traffic. The delays which have taken place in connection with the construction of the extension – a work which has been on hand for 11 years or more – have been many and vexatious, but at last the stigma of being shut out from the world in respect of having no railway communication is removed from Cardigan. On Tuesday morning a train of six ordinary coaches and one saloon, with two vans, left Whitland at about 10.45 am, having on board Mr. H. Besant, the divisional superintendent of the GWR and other officials and visitors. Cardigan was reached at about 1 pm, and the party were received on the platform by the Mayor (Mr. T. Davies, Bank House) the members of the corporation, and a very large number of the inhabitants.

At this point on this "auspicious day", the Mayor launched into a distinctly florid speech of welcome to Mr. Besant and the railway. *The South Wales Daily News* then reported that "at half past one the directors of the W & C. R. entertained a number of visitors to the luncheon, which was provided by Mr. Trollip in the goods shed at the station. Colonel Lewis of Clynfiew presided." The great and the good of the district, together with railway officials and engineers, were duly wined and dined, before the chairman proposed a toast: "Success to the Whitland & Cardigan Railway".

A local shareholder and resident Mr. C. Morgan Richardson responded, and thanked the directors for the result of their ten years work. His other comments reflected not only the deeply felt importance of the day for Cardigan, but also an undue optimism about future prospects. In his view "That day they had wiped out a great disgrace, and tomorrow no one could say that there was one county town in England or Wales without a railway. (Applause). But they must not stop at Cardigan. They must carry the line down to the sea, and make a great Irish trade. To this end they must clear their river, and improve their port. (Applause).

The chairman acknowledged a great debt of gratitude to the GWR, because without their "powerful assistance.....the line would have been stuck at a little place beyond Kilgerran", and proposed a toast "Success to the Great Western Railway". Responding, Mr. Besant pointed out that previously, in the absence of a railway, many people did not know of the many local attractions. He added that he "had no doubt at all that the opening of the line would increase business in the town of Cardigan and the district generally". The Engineer, J.B. Walton, responded to a personal toast by making a very appropriate expression of regret "that the late chairman John Owen had not been permitted to see that day". The Mayor then concluded the speeches by announcing that the GWR planned to run an excursion from Cardigan to London on September 10th!

According to *The South Wales Daily News*:- "the return train left Cardigan at about 3.30pm, and a large crowd witnessed its departure. In the evening a public dinner was held to celebrate the event, and on the next evening (September 1st) the festivities concluded with a banquet given by the Mayor of Cardigan to the Corporation and other friends."

Before World War I

The history of the three Whitland & Cardigan locomotives has been described. As regards rolling stock, it appears that few (if any) of the W&CR vehicles survived long in Great Western ownership. Certainly this was true of the carriages. The GWR allotted numbers 6597/8 to the two composites, and numbers 1669/70/1/2 to the four thirds, but quickly condemned them in April, 1887, without even recording their dimensions. A story that one of these carriages became a van for otter hounds has been doubted. The GWR built a hounds van in 1887, but it bore no similarity to a W&CR carriage. In the Edwardian era the GWR and several other companies sold redundant carriage bodies to private buyers, and some ended up in West Wales. Most

Llanglydwen station May 2019. *Author*

Civic dignitaries and other guests at Login station for the opening of the 'Cardi Bach' museum 14th May, 2019. *Author*

became small dwellings situated near the coast, but a few found their way into the Taf valley. For a few years after the closure of the railway, two were to be seen close to the former quarry siding at Glogue. At the time of writing only one is known to survive at an extremely isolated location about a mile from Llanfyrnach.

At the time of opening Crymmych Arms had a passing loop, but only one platform for regular passenger use. Plainly this was a constraint on the service, and at the beginning of 1896 the GWR asked the Board of Trade to approve the renewal of the loop on the down side, the provision of a proper platform, waiting shed and signal box, the rearrangement of the siding connections, and the re-signalling of the entire site. The plan then provided a signal box with 21 levers, but the box that was built contained 23 levers, of which 4 were spare. The 1 in 35 gradient on the approach to Crymmych Arms from the south was always a matter for concern, and the Board of Trade asserted that:- "Owing to the gradient, no goods train should be allowed to approach the place from the direction of Whitland unless the down home signal can be lowered to permit the train to run into the loop, and get inside the catch points without coming to a stand on the single line".

In brief, no one wanted a train to stall on the running line when approaching Crymmych, and for safety's sake it was deemed inappropriate for another train to be in the station at the same time. This provision became the cause of considerable delays. In August, 1912, those delays averaged 11 minutes per up train, and 12 minutes two months later – because under these arrangements up trains had to wait at Boncath before coming forward to Crymmych Arms. The Great Western wanted up trains to be allowed to proceed as far as the up home signal to the north of Crymmych Arms, and also proposed the use of 20 ton brakevans on the Cardigan line in place of the less robust brakevans usually used on local freight services. In early 1913 this was agreed by the Board of Trade. (MT6 2159/2).

Later in 1913 the GWR decided that the siding at Rhydowen should become a goods loop by the installation of points at the south end of the station. Colonel van Donop inspected the work for the Board of Trade in January, 1914, and apart from the need to fit a disc signal with a red light, deemed it satisfactory. (MT6 2254/8). This change was almost certainly not connected with a very brief revival in wartime of the narrow gauge Penlan tramway for forestry purposes. In 1916 the GWR advised the Board of Trade of their wish to do similar work at Llanfyrnach, turning the siding north of the station into a goods loop, thereby enabling the practice of tow-roping wagons to be abolished. This was agreed, and the work was inspected on 6th December, 1916, by Colonel J.W.Pringle, who noted that the points and facing point locks were controlled from a new North End ground frame, controlled by the key on the electric train staff. (There was already a gate box adjoining the level crossing). Once again concern was expressed about the working of goods trains on gradients. Col. Pringle observed that "Owing to the gradient it will be necessary for all goods trains to have attached to them a 20 ton brakevan, and the working instructions should include a direction to Guards to pin down 25% of wagons before the siding is worked." (MT6 2430/4).

After World War I

The Great Western pioneered the operation of country bus services in conjunction with local rail passenger trains, two of the earliest instances in Wales being road motor services between Aberayron (another anglicised spelling) and Lampeter, and Aberayron and Aberystwyth, both in 1906. The dispersed towns and villages in West Wales seemed well-suited to such operations, and in the summer of 1911 Cardigan had the benefit of GWR bus services to both Newcastle Emlyn and Fishguard. The initial arrangement appears to have been short-lived, but in the 1920's Cardigan became a significant focus for GWR road services, not only to Newcastle Emlyn and Fishguard, but also to New Quay, Aberayron and Aberystwyth. Although these services were intended primarily for local people, visitors were not overlooked, and for a time it was possible to purchase a 5/- one-day runabout ticket for use on any of the relevant buses. The success of the Great Western services became a concern to other private bus operators, but an Act of 1928 allowed the GWR to negotiate better arrangements with them. This suited the Great Western, and by 1933 the services radiating out from Cardigan had been transferred to the Western Welsh Omnibus Co.

In 1926 an enjoyable but somewhat controversial book was published entitled *The South Wales Squires*. The author, Herbert M. Vaughan, himself a member of the squirearchy, referred to the Taf valley as being "a most remote and little explored region" in which "the Church is very weak. Dissent is embittered and all powerful", He then described the railway as "a wretched branch line from Whitland to Cardigan, detested locally for its tedium, delays and shakiness." As a man of the world, undoubtedly he had seen better, but if the criticism was harsh, it was not entirely unfounded. In the early years, especially, the Whitland & Cardigan was not exactly a by-word for comfort and security. The late E.T. Lewis, who knew the district intimately, once wrote about an overweight man who felt it prudent to move his bulk from one side of the carriage to the other as it ran above precipitous drops on the steeply graded descent towards Cardigan.

By the early twentieth century Whitland was easily the largest settlement in the ancient parishes of Llanboidy and Llangan, but it was not until 1930 that it was recognised as a separate and distinct parish. This was long overdue. By 1935 no less than 350 people were being employed at Whitland by the GWR in assorted aspects of railway operation, and not least the locomotive shed and nearby shunting yards. The milk factory belonging to United Dairies, first opened in 1911 under the auspices of the Somerset & South Wales Dairies, provided employment for over 200 more. The late Ray Bowen, born in Whitland in 1927, gave a vivid account of this busy junction in its heyday, in about 1938:

> In the long down bay platform stood an open- cabbed 19xx pannier tank. It was dwarfed by the one composite coach which made up the entire train. The engine was shining clean, the crew idly surveying the scene, knowing that they

had some time before following the winding River Taf into the Preseli Hills, eventually reaching Cardigan – which was a long 'tomorrow will do' distance away. Immediately in front stood the Pembroke & Tenby train (P & T) composed of two 'B' set coaches, and headed by a truly resplendent 45xx class prairie tank.....(As the westbound train for Neyland groaned to a stand alongside) ... ..the doors burst open, yielding all manner of human society. Porters shouted 'Cross the platform for the P&T train!' 'P&T train in front!' The P&T had ceased to exist in 1897! Sadistic porters, to confuse Anglo-Saxon travellers, would shout in Welsh "Change for Carmarthen. Cardi Bach in the rear!' Mountains of grey mail bags tumbled out onto waiting trolleys. Stacks of parcels of unbelievable height were placed on trolleys to advance slowly and cautiously, like medieval siege engines, to be placed against the wide open double doors of our train. More crashes, bangs and shouts. The theory that you cannot get more than a pint into a pint pot was totally disproved as the parcels and bags disappeared into the seemingly far too small space afforded by the composite coach.

At this period Ray Bowen's father was a driver at Whitland, and although the GWR was a well-regulated company, railwaymen did not regard the "Cardi Bach" with all the seriousness that might have been expected; at Whitland shed any leisurely job was often described as "banking the Boncath". On the Cardigan branch the rule book was not followed in every particular. At the crossing place of Llanglydwen, 'up' trains heading for Whitland usually had to wait several minutes for the arrival of the 'down' train for Cardigan, and the 'up' service might well gain time down the gradients from Crymmych Arms Accordingly enginemen had an understanding with the landlord of the Penybont Inn, whereby when the 'up' train was within 100 yards of the station the driver would sound his whistle once, twice or even three times to tell the landlord how many pints of beer he should pull! A very detailed account of Great Western freight operations and traffic was given by Stanley Jenkins and Chris Turner in the *Great Western Journal*, No. 30, (Spring, 1999, p.302). Not surprisingly, most of the traffic was agricultural – cattle and pigs being a particular feature on the last Tuesday of the month, being market day at Crymmych Arms. This same well-illustrated article also includes some brief but fascinating reminiscences by former members of staff at both Cardigan and Crymmych Arms, providing a more complete picture of activity along the line in later years.

Tank locomotives of the 850 and 19xx classes were used on Cardigan branch services up to the 1940's, those employed including Nos. 1910, 1979, 1996 and 2018. The 45xx and 4575 class 2-6-2 tank engines reached Whitland in the 1930's, primarily for work on the former Pembroke & Tenby route, but do not seem to have been used on the Cardigan line before 1941. In addition to those already noted, it is known that 4506, 4513, 4515, 4519, 4541, 4551, 4553, 4556, 4558, 4576, 4579, 4594, 5520, 5526, 5527, 5529, 5546, 5549, and 5551 were used at different periods. Later in the 1950's pannier tanks in the 16xx series were often seen on the branch, including 1611, 1613, 1628, 1638, 1643, 1644, and 1659. The locomotive shed at Llanelly had a sizeable allocation of these tank locomotives, including some of those listed here, which suggests that sometimes they may, in effect, have been loaned to Whitland for use on the Cardigan branch.

The most famous passenger ever carried by the "Cardi Bach" was Winston Churchill, on Good Friday, 11th April, 1941. He was accompanied by his wife, and daughter Mary, and by John Winant (the United States ambassador), Lord Ismay and various defence officials and civil servants. Unfortunately no photograph, or even record of this train has emerged, but the rolling stock was surely better and more substantial than usual, and the train quite possibly double-headed. Presumably a water stop at Glogue would have been required before the train continued to Cardigan, from where the party proceeded by road to Aberporth, where they evidently witnessed a "noisy but interesting display of rockets and U.P. projectiles." Being wartime, no publicity was given to this excursion, and it is difficult to be certain of the exact facts. According to one unverified version of the story, Churchill also visited a large, isolated house near Boncath which had been requisitioned (it is said) for secret scientific research. What is much more certain is that the party returned to Whitland, and spent the night on the Prime Minister's main line train. The next day the train took them on to Bristol, where Churchill endeavoured to bring encouragement to a city hard hit by bombing.

As mentioned in the text, G.Cohen Ltd was granted the contract to lift the line, and work began very late in 1963. They made their base at Llanglydwen, a station which provided sufficient space for the storage of track panels and the sorting of track components. It appears that Cohens made no use of the main line connection with British Railways, and so began by lifting from Taf Vale Junction, and working north. This contract provided Cohens with some re-usable track panels and many steel sleepers, but as the track in the sidings was virtually life-expired a subsidiary contract for their disposal (relating to the length from Login to Kilgerran) was given to a local farmer and businessman named Dewi Owen. Whereas Cohens imported a small diesel locomotive to assist their work (perhaps the only diesel ever to work on the branch), Dewi Owen devised a much more remarkable vehicle – an ancient Austin 10 adapted to run on the railway.

After the railway had closed Dewi had purchased the Station House at Crymmych Arms (then devoid of mains services) for £500. Like many people in North Pembrokeshire, he was not prosperous, but he was practical, and able to make the most of whatever he had. The road wheels on the Austin 10 were replaced (apparently) by the wheel sets from a track maintenance trolley, thereby lowering the gearing, and enabling the car to handle heavier loads at low speed. A steel bar on a pivot provide a coupling with another maintenance trolley, which actually carried the sleepers or track components. This rather ramshackle ensemble was used mostly between Cohen's base at Llanglydwen and Dewi's home at Crymmych, although it is thought to have gone south to Login at least once, and occasionally north to Cardigan when Dewi had business in the town. As the main track lifting contract was completed in late July, 1964 (the sidings at Crymmych possibly lasting a little longer) Dewi's unconventional railcar had a working life of no more than twelve months. In the autumn of 1964 a couple of visitors from London inspected the machine, and apparently bought it as a curiosity for a private museum. Unfortunately in 2013 Anne James, Dewi's daughter (since sadly deceased) could not recall the location of the museum, but it must be doubtful if the car still exists.

Inevitably the passage of time has seen changes along the route of the "Cardi Bach". For those who know where to look when travelling west of Whitland by train, the site of Cardigan Junction is just discernible, but any visitor to Llanfalteg now hoping to find the former station will look in vain. The site has been cleared, and housing erected where once there was a station building. Alongside, though, a rough track passes behind the housing and leads onto the former trackbed. Further north, the rather isolated crossing keeper's lodge at Penclippen is occupied, and as already mentioned, Login station is inhabited and home to the "Cardi Bach" museum. In time to come Carmarthenshire County Council hope to create a public footpath on their portion of the old railway from Llanfalteg to Rhydowen, and at the time of writing the section from Login to Llanglydwen seems the most likely to benefit. Llanglydwen station has altered little over the past thirty years, but in 2019 the nearby Penybont Inn appeared to have closed. At Rhydowen all trace of the former station has been erased, although the adjoining station house has been modernised, and a rather unusual hemispherical extension added on the end abutting onto the adjoining minor road. Ironically, part of the alignment of the former Penlan tramway near Aberelwyn Farm now constitutes a little-used public footpath.

Beyond Rhydowen the valley of the Taf is in Pembrokeshire, and approaching Llanfyrnach the former trackbed serves as a field access. The station building at Llanfyrnach is now a private house behind a high hedge and substantial fencing. North of the station the old goods yard and adjoining land serve as a lorry park for vehicles belonging to the busy local haulage firm of Mansel Davies & Son Ltd. In contrast, the once important quarries and water stop at Glogue has become a quiet and sleepy hamlet near the head of the valley. The water tank has gone, the platform edge has been thoroughly eroded, and the trackbed partially infilled. Only the station house and the remnant of a crossing gate remain. Inevitably the quarries are prominent, but one of the quarry pits has become a refuse tip.

At Crymmych Arms the station house has seen some alterations and extensions, but now provides a residence with pleasant views to the east. A small trading estate with modern buildings has been created in the goods yard, and part is a public car park. The cutting to the north of the road bridge has been infilled for at least fifty yards, and parts of the trackbed beyond are heavily overgrown. In 2019 the former station building at Boncath was still standing, although badly decayed. The rest of the site could be described as a wilderness, with some parking at one side. Three miles further north, below the long 1 in 40 descent from Boncath, the scene at Kilgerran, was little better. Here the station had been erased, and the land used as a car park and store yard by a builders' merchant. North of Kilgerran much of the trackbed is now an unadopted road through the Teifi Marshes Reserve, a beautiful area of reeds and wetland on the south side of the River Teifi. The old station building at Cardigan was demolished in 1990, but the nearby goods shed stands, still supporting an awning thought to date from 1947. It is hard to believe that this one older building surrounded by many unremarkable sheds in a trading estate, could have been the setting for a grand lunch party at the opening of the line on 31st August, 1886!

In spite of its limitations, there can be no doubt that at a time when roads were poor, and private transport a privilege, the 'Cardi Bach' provided a valuable link with the rest of the world. It had real commercial significance for many more than just the Glogue quarries, and the Boncath Mercantile Co. It served farmers, shopkeepers and tradespeople in all the little communities along the route, and in winter it could be a positive lifeline. H.M.Vaughan was particularly impressed by the traffic in rabbits. "At every station" he wrote "the platform is covered with crates upon crates of stiffened rabbits ready to be dispatched to large towns, chiefly in the North of England". Even in 1962 the present writer was fascinated to see the railway's social significance: packages conveyed from one station to another, news and jokes exchanged in Welsh rather than English, and housewives making their way to and from Cardigan, or Whitland (for connections to Carmarthen).

The closure of the 'Cardi Bach' brought a way of life to an end. This was illustrated most clearly in a feature published in the *Western Telegraph* in October, 1982. Describing the village of Glogue, it concluded with some reflections given by Haydn Davies, Glogue Shop: "People started buying clocks", said Mr. Davies. "Before, their whole day revolved around the trains which passed through. They got up when the 7.30am arrived, had lunch when the goods passed up to Cardigan, and went to bed when they heard the last train. A whole pattern of life changed." Although that way of life has gone, the area remains as Welsh as ever, and the railway is commemorated in a local Welsh language newspaper entitled the *Cardi Bach*. For its many years of service the 'Cardi Bach' – charming, tiresome and idiosyncratic - deserves its special place in local history.

Appendix
Passenger Services 1910–1958

Bradshaw's timetable April 1910